To Curtis
I appreciate your
support

FINANCIAL FOUNDATIONS

Building Financial Freedom
One Tool At A Time

LARESE PURNELL

Financial Foundations: Building Financial Freedom One Tool at a Time

Scripture quotations marked (NASB) are taken from the NEW AMERICAN STANDARD BIBLE®, Copyright © 1960,1962,1963,1968,1971,1972,1973,1975,1977,1995 by The Lockman Foundation. Used by permission.

Scripture quotations marked (NLT) are taken from the Holy Bible, New Living Translation, copyright © 1996, 2004, 2007 by Tyndale House Foundation. Used by permission of Tyndale House Publishers, Inc., Carol Stream, Illinois 60188. All rights reserved.

ISBN-10: 0615960235
ISBN-13: 978-0-615-96023-4

Victory Media & Publishing Company
16781 Chagrin Boulevard #132
Cleveland, OH 44120
www.victorymp.com

pandpconsulting2@gmail.com

Follow *@laresepurnell* on Twitter and Instagram

Printed in the USA

CONTENTS

———

DEDICATION

Above all, to my Heavenly Father. Everything I am is because of You Lord. Thank You for the knowledge and wisdom You've allowed me to acquire throughout the years. I will not hoard this information; instead, I will share my knowledge with others. It is my prayer that they receive this information and avoid many common financial pitfalls because of it. I pray that those who read this book that are dedicated to change will experience Your financial blessings.

I dedicate this book to my family. To my childhood sweetheart and best friend Tiesha, my daughter Gabriella, and to my son Gaven. Thank you for your support and sacrifices, which have made it possible for me to do the work God has called me to do. Tiesha, without your guidance and persistent help, this book would not have been possible. Life has not always been easy, but we've made it through. Thank you for standing by my side. I will be forever grateful. Gabbi and Gaven, thank you for loving me unconditionally. Everything that I set forth to accomplish is to ensure you are able to live a wonderful life. Keep being the amazing children you already are.

To Dr. R. A. Vernon, Founder and Senior Pastor of the greatest church in the nation, "THE WORD" Church; my pastor, CEO, and mentor, I appreciate you for pushing me to break generational curses, not only financially, but in all areas of my life. Thank you for exposing me to new levels. I am a better man, husband, and father because God saw fit for us to cross paths. I appreciate you for pushing me to think big. I am grateful that you inspired me to reach for greater. Thank you for providing me an opportunity to be an integral part of your organization at such a young age. I am proud to say that I get to be the Chief Financial Officer and Chief of Staff of "THE WORD" Church.

To my loving mother, I appreciate you for always speaking into my life. You've always told me I could be great; you've always pushed me to be better. Also, I thank you for giving me all those book title ideas during noon Bible study.

To my staff, friends, family members, and brothers and sisters in Christ, thank you for all of your support and encouragement throughout the years.

Sincere gratitude is hereby extended again to my wife, Tiesha Purnell, and Jennifer Wainwright of Text Tweaker. Each of you were vital to the completion of this book. If it weren't for the both of you, no one would be reading this right now. I do not take for granted all of the long hours and research it took to complete this project. I truly appreciate you ladies. Thank you!

FOREWORD

I know firsthand what it's like to grow up in poverty and be forced to overcome a myriad of emotional, mental, and financial barriers to achieve success. As a result, I feel compelled to share what I've learned to help others accomplish their goals and become their best selves. I am a longtime advocate of building relationships and believe in teaching others the power of capitalizing on their skills and gifts to connect to the world around them. As an African American, I especially have a heart for those with whom I share a common ancestry and desire to see them create wealth for themselves, leave legacies for their families, and through their service, sacrifice, and information-sharing, have a lasting impact on their communities.

To that end, I think LaRese's *Financial Foundations* is an invaluable resource for those who desire change in their lives and want to be better financial stewards. The principles he shares align with what I believe will propel people to the promise of personal and professional prosperity and help them and their posterity steer clear of the impoverished mindsets that often breed hardship and peril. He advocates financial literacy and self-empowerment through knowledge acquisition, accountability, and individual responsibility and is doing his part to see to it that we can all live the lives we aim to live by teaching us the inherent authority of sound money management.*Financial Foundations* is a smart read that not only brings financial issues to the forefront, but breaks them down in the simplest of terms making it easy to apply and share the advice. Take it from me: if you want to take control of your financial wellbeing and secure your future and the future of those whom you love, you need to read this book and refer to it often when you feel less than motivated to be disciplined with your money. I am honored and privileged to lend my voice and support to such a worthy, necessary cause.

Dr. George C. Fraser
Chairman and CEO of FraserNet, Inc.

PREFACE

If I were putting together a short list of the most important people in my life, LaRese Purnell would easily make it. As a man of faith I believe some individuals are divinely placed in your life as participants in your overall destiny. Without question he is such a person in my life and the life of "THE WORD" Church. When he came on staff, we, like many mega churches, had the good problem of growing faster than we could keep up with financially. Although offerings were great, our overhead was greater. Between facility costs, a growing staff and trying to meet the needs of a poor city, we found ourselves in a financial conundrum.

One of my staff members mentioned to me that there was a young man serving in our parking ministry who worked at a local bank and had an MBA in finance. Although he was young, he had a good feeling about him. In all honesty, because of so much turnover in the CFO position for reasons that would take up the rest of my allotted space in this wonderful book, I was quite hesitant and maybe even a bit pessimistic about the proposition of bringing him aboard. After a careful vetting process and much prayer I decided to pull the trigger and hire LaRese Purnell as our Chief Financial Officer.

I knew he was different and that something big was happening when he and I met to discuss his starting salary. I was taken aback when he refused to accept the generous offer I made him, citing that I had overpaid in the past and had not gotten the best results. He asked me to pay him less and give him a year to turn us around financially and then we could discuss an increase in salary. Not before or since has any employee (and understandably so) asked to be paid less until they proved their worth to our ministry.

I'm proud to say that a year later he and my Chief of Staff at the time, Stacy Collins, who has since started his own profitable managing company, literally turned us around financially and we have not looked back. Not long after, that LaRese took on the dual role of Chief Financial Officer/Chief of Staff and has done a masterful job of conflating the two and earning a reputation across the nation as one of the top young executives to keep your eyes on.

What he's done for our church in and of itself is noteworthy, what he's done for my family and me in terms of financial stabilization is immeasurable. He is absolutely my number one. He handles all of my personal business ventures and financial undertakings. Simply put, the man understands finance and business. This book will help everyone from a high-level CEO to the average Joe just trying to keep his head above water financially.

In his first literary undertaking, LaRese has shown that he is one of the up and coming special talents in the area of business and money. I'm blessed to have him as my right-hand man who has kept not only our church, but me personally in financial compliance and has never shown anything but the highest integrity handling the millions of dollars that have passed through our ministry. This book is a must read for anyone serious about financial freedom and generational wealth. I'm an eyewitness that his strategies are proven and trustworthy. Not since Dave Ramsey have I been this impressed with such a beautiful financial mind.

In His Name,

R. A. Vernon, D.Min.
Founder and Senior Pastor of "THE WORD" Church

FINANCIAL QUOTATIONS

───────

We all want wealth, but how do we earn it? While there are plenty of ways to build wealth, for most of us, this means we'll need a successful career. To have a successful career, we need to refine skills, develop talents, and acquire knowledge that makes us more valuable than the next person competing for the same or a similar profession, and of course, a little favor and good fortune doesn't hurt.

Invest in yourself by getting an education. Read books that improve your mind and increase your knowledge base. Secure a quality job where you can learn superior, marketable skills. Identify your gifts and abilities and go to work finding a way to turn them into an income generating vehicle. Comb the internet for creative business ideas. There are thousands of professional blogs created by entrepreneurs who lend their creativity and expertise to others seeking to build their own wealth. Much of the information shared online is free; some is not. Search for credible, proven sources, follow them, and capitalize on what they've learned to help you strengthen your personal brand, build your own business, or come up with your own idea for making money. In doing so, you can truly leverage your career or business into an engine of your wealth.

If you're a millionaire by the time you're thirty, but blow it by the time your forty, you've gained nothing. Grow and protect your investment portfolio by carefully diversifying it, and you may find yourself in a position to prep your posterity for wealth as well. (If you don't know what an investment portfolio is or you don't know how to get one started, you're reading the right book).

"Financial peace isn't the acquisition of stuff. It's learning to live on less than you make, so you can give money back and have money to invest. You can't win until you do this." – Dave Ramsey

By being modest in your spending, you can insulate yourself and your family against numerous problems related to credit card debt, collection accounts, and not having enough money for emergency situations. You will also have enough for retirement if you're scrupulous and smart in your financial planning practices and can give back to empower your local community as well.

"I will tell you how to become rich. Be fearful when others are greedy. Be greedy when others are fearful." – Warren Buffet

It would do you good to embrace the financial mind of Warren Buffet; be prepared to invest in a down market and to get out in a soaring market.

A POETIC WORD

———

Basheer Jones

Your condition will never change until you first change your mind

If that never changes then you will always remain behind

Whatever you want in life believe me you can have it. It's not magic.

You must change your thoughts, which in turn will change your habits.

But, people just focus on increasing their dollars and that's so tragic.

Because the dreams that they see they can never grab it.

Don't focus on just making money; let's build wealth.

But before we do that we must first build self.

Making money shouldn't be the only part to the mission.

Change your mindset and with that you'll change your condition.

INTRODUCTION

———

Bridge to Financial Freedom

Every day that I wake up, I thank God for delivering me from the mindset of poverty. I grew up poor, as so many have. My mother was a single parent struggling through the system of welfare. We'd even been placed in a shelter or two in the Cleveland area with nowhere else to lay our heads. At times, I even had to live with various family members, having to change school districts and meet new friends on many occasions.

Yet, despite the circumstances I grew up in, I was determined to make it to college and graduate; which brought its own set of financial struggles. I didn't understand the power of money then, however, I was determined to live a more balanced and successful life than the one I'd grown up in. I was never given the foundation of good financial stewardship, as my family didn't have it to give. So, when I arrived on that college campus, bombarded with "free" credit cards, t-shirt giveaways, and gift cards, immediately I found myself signing up for everything available. Weeks later multiple cards arrived in my mailbox with limits beginning at $1000.

Add to that, I was introduced to payday loans, which made my financial situation worse. Sometimes I had multiple loans outstanding all at once, just to pay for books and monthly housing bills. This began a cycle of debt that took me years to climb out of. I bought things I couldn't afford and lived beyond my means. Not knowing at times psychologically, I was trying to make up for things I never had the opportunity or experience to buy growing up.

Not having the appropriate financial foundation caused me to adopt money habits that were passed down in my family throughout generations. Debt. Bad credit. No money. Poverty mentality. I did what I saw others close to me do, whether it was normal or not. Parents keep in mind that your kids watch everything you do, even how you handle your finances.

By the time I graduated from college, I still had not grasped the concept of financial freedom; however, when I had children, a new level of responsibility was birthed within me. The training I received through my college coursework and through my work experiences started to make sense. I realized that I wanted more for myself, my wife, and my children. I was ready to break generational curses related to money and although it still took several more years to do so, I embraced my financial freedom and worked very hard to achieve it. I didn't have help in my quest to reach financial tranquility. I realized no one in my family had the resources to assist me when I'd hit my financial rock-bottom. I knew then that I had to become the Daniel of my family. As a member of the newer generation it was my responsibility to change the course of not only my future, but that of my family's as well.

I will never forget a college classmate of mine, Justin. We graduated together and both received job offers from the same financial institution. In conversation one day we were discussing finances. Not bragging, he shared with me his financial portfolio. He had over $30,000 and we were only twenty-two years old. At that time I had less than $500 in my account. I was blown away at his sophistication with investing and saving. He talked about how he was trained by his parents to save money since he was a kid. His parents would encourage him to save 25 percent of all birthday money, Christmas cash, and once he got a job in high school, paychecks until he went to college. He continued what he was taught through college. The amount he had saved was after paying for his brand new car, cash! I am sharing this with you because it proves when you are educated and you create good habits, it impacts your circumstances.

Over the years, I have assisted many individuals with creating a plan for financial freedom. The first thing I tell them is, "It starts with you." You have to be disciplined with your finances and dedicated in your efforts for change to occur. My hope is to help you lay a foundation for your finances that you can build on.

If you read this information and don't apply it, you will have wasted your time. Utilize this book as a tool, one that you can reach for whenever you need inspiration to get your *money matters* in order. (Thank you, Dr. Vernon).

Dr. Vernon (who you'll hear me reference frequently—the man is a walking wealth of wisdom) teaches that money matters. Every year, he spends an entire month or so teaching on finance and the issues that accompany money mismanagement. He also explains how having money and handling it well can put you in a powerful position to help, influence, and give to others. *Money Matters* is a comprehensive overview about all things money, starting with what the Bible says. The entire series is available at www.wordcity.org. One of Dr. Vernon's favorite phrases is that everyone has a blind spot. If finances are in yours, then I highly recommend you get this series.

Ask any architect and they will tell you the most important step when constructing a home or building is drawing the blueprint so you can provide a plan for the construction team. Then, the next step and most important stage is laying a proper foundation. The same is true with your finances. You have to lay a concrete financial foundation before you can frame your fiscal future, build wealth, or gain access to financial freedom. If you don't have fundamental principles in place guiding your daily decisions with respect to your money, your financial situation will eventually crumble.

This is why you see athletes, movie stars, and well-to-do family members gain wealth and lose it all. Their core beliefs about finance are faulty and they don't understand how to manage their money. You must become financially literate and educate yourself regarding the power of money in order to successfully handle—and grow— your finances.

As you continue to read, you'll observe that there is an extensive amount of information in this book. However, though extensive, the information is practical. The goal of this book is to provide all readers, no matter what your current financial status, with knowledge that will help you on your road to financial fortitude. Or, to borrow a commonly voiced phrase from no-nonsense money guru Dave Ramsey, to help you reach "financial peace."

Finance is an area that we are either working on, ignoring, repairing, restructuring, or attempting to shift to another level. My objective is to provide you with the information necessary to move your finances to a greater plane where success is inevitable. My intention is to challenge you to clearly understand your current financial status. And let's be clear: not only do you need to know your money and money habits inside and out, you need to understand how money works, period. You need to understand the difference between simple and compound interest, what a 529 Plan is if you have kids, and how to cut years off your mortgage by paying the same amount, twice a month. Know the importance of educating yourself in every area of money from investing to saving to debt management.

When you're finished reading this book, use it as a consistent reference whenever you have questions about money. If I've done a good job (and you don't try to read this when you're sleepy), you should be able to explain the financial concepts you've learned with others when asked. *Financial Foundations* is going to help you create a roadmap so that you can construct financial goals, accomplish those goals, and then set new goals as your financial situation improves. Setting monetary goals is an important part of the process as this will keep you motivated as you pursue financial freedom.

Throughout Dr. Vernon's teachings, he's stated that a person cannot become saved, join the kingdom of believers, and then within five months expect all of their wrongs for the past twenty-five years to be wiped away immediately. That same idea applies to your present financial situation. Once you decide that you want to get your finances in order, it will take time, patience, and commitment before you can clear years of irresponsible money decisions. However, don't fret or get frustrated. Peace and joy will come as you embrace the notion that laying and strengthening a financial foundation is a process. Anything worth having requires hard work, and no doubt about it, this will be hard work!

When you are able to put your newly acquired financial tools to work, you'll feel great. If you're married, your marriage will improve as financial stressors are lessened. If you have children, you'll worry a little less when you know you have a plan for their college education. If you're single but under a mountain of debt, you'll feel better when you can at least begin to see how you're going to shave a little off that mountain every month until it's nothing more than a molehill.

Each area of your life can be affected by finances, or lack thereof… Wait…who am I kidding? Let me be real with you. Each area of your life *is* affected by your finances, or lack thereof. When you care about quality, substance, and excellence, money dictates everything from the type of food you eat and the clothes you wear, to the home you live in and the school your kids go to—but again, no need to worry. You're reading this book and that's a huge step in the right direction. If you implement the tools and internalize the principles I give you, the discipline you'll create from reading this book alone will encourage you in all facets of your life.

Now, what else can you expect from *Financial Foundations*? We'll address the "do's" and "don'ts" concerning your credit. There's plenty of (wrong) information out there about credit and we're going to clear up the most common misconceptions. We'll also discuss the importance of both cash and credit as necessary monetary mediums. Yep. You read that right. Credit is a necessary monetary medium. (In my opinion obviously; it is my book, right?)

Seriously, that might sound a little strange considering I quoted Dave Ramsey only a few pages ago and the Bible appears to discourage debt. However, without getting into a debate about Dave's doctrine or a theological tiff over biblical interpretation, let's just say there are many different ways to approach fixing your finances and depending on worldview, culture, and experiences of the one offering advice the solutions you'll hear to solving your issues will differ from person to person. As far as the Bible is concerned, I believe the Word dissuades the inappropriate use of credit because of the spiritual, emotional, and mental repercussions of being overwhelmingly in debt. But, we'll table this discussion for now and get back to my original point—cash and credit are not mutually exclusive. I will inform you of what you need to know so that you can make responsible economic decisions.

Moreover, you will learn how to create a manageable budget, one that won't have you sneaking behind your own back to break because it's unrealistic. If you're trying to feed a family of five then you have to allot more than $100 a month for groceries, unless of course you're one of those connoisseur coupon clippers who knows when and where to shop and what to buy at what time. (I am amazed by how much those savvy shoppers on The Learning Channel's *Extreme Couponing* save in a grocery store trip). But, for most of us who don't have the time, won't make the time, or just don't care to spend the time couponing, you need a sensible budget you won't have a problem sticking to. I'll show you how to make one.

Also, I'll tell you the people you should build relationships with to create successful financial affairs. The people in your financial circle are almost as important to your success as you are. I know you've heard this before—it's all about who you know. Knowing the right people gives you access to the right information at the right time. For example, if you get a letter in the mail from the IRS about an impending wage garnishment because of past due taxes (God forbid), you're not going to want to call your mother. Well, you may, but chances are unless she's a tax expert, she'll be able to do little more than lend you a shoulder to cry on and recommend that you call one.

If you get a windfall of money from a long-lost uncle and you want to invest it wisely, telling your persuasive best friend who has yet *another* unproven business idea is probably not the best thing to do. Strong financial partnerships and fiscally responsible relationships are important no matter what your financial stage and status. I'm going to tell you whose numbers you should have saved in your favorites so you'll know just who to call when you're in a tough money situation.

As you begin the journey, keep this quote in mind, "Defeat doesn't finish a man, quit does. A man is not finished when he's defeated. He's finished when he quits." - Richard M. Nixon

1

THE BLUEPRINT

—

The Basics of Budgeting

But don't begin until you count the cost. For who would begin construction of a building without first calculating the cost to see if there is enough money to finish it? (Luke 14:28 NLT)

Answer these question: Does your pants pocket or purse currently contain your entire life's savings? Moreover, are you living paycheck to paycheck? If your answer to these two questions is yes, I bet that your life is flying by as you await your next paycheck. Life should be about so much more than waiting for the funds to pay your monthly expenses, which, by the way, most of you are drowning in. This adds unnecessary stress to your life. Not to mention, it is not God's will for your life. He wants you to have peace, joy, and margin in all areas, including your finances.

It is common knowledge that financial struggles are one of the most common reasons for divorce. According to an article by Ron Leiber of the New York Times in 2009, the odds of a marriage ending in divorce due to finances is approximately 45 percent. Research has proven that number to be consistent over past decades. The lack of money leads to the demise of many relationships. During one of his many teachings on the subject, Dr. Vernon indicated that when you have "no money," every argument with your spouse, no matter the topic, ends with, "...and we don't have no money!" It could have been an argument about what you had for dinner or not being able to find the remote control, but rest assured it will always end with the mutual understanding that you're broke.

So, take accountability for your current situation and give God some tools to work with. Be mindful of the fact that you got yourself in this situation; work hard to get yourself out of it. Stop blaming the people around you and taking your frustrations out on them. There is nothing wrong with making mistakes out of ignorance. And sure, many times, making some minor mistakes when you do know better won't kill you (although it's just plain old dumb to make a mistake knowing it's a mistake). Just make sure you learn from those experiences and apply the lesson learned to minimize the likelihood of you having to revisit a similar situation. Ignorance is not just the absence of knowledge; it's revisiting the same issue continually (or maybe that's idiocy).

Knowing where you stand in any area of your life allows you to plan and prepare for the future. As the saying goes, "If you fail to plan, you plan to fail." In many cases, we don't like to acknowledge our current status in the areas of our lives that we're most negligent in or just don't understand. So we ignore the situation (Ever notice that ignore is the root word of ignorant?) and live day to day instead of thinking of the future. The only way to get the answers we need to move forward is to first acknowledge our situation, evaluate it, commit to educating ourselves, and then decide and dedicate ourselves to being better.

Tired of not being able to answer your phone or allowing your kids to pick up and tell everyone you're not home, while sitting right next to them and the phone? Stop hanging up on bill collectors. No one should be a prisoner in their own home or on their own line. It's important to understand that not dealing with our issues or avoiding them, financial or otherwise, will only make the situation worse or stagnate. Remember that retail credit card you ran up in college? Well, you may choose to "forget" that debt but I guarantee you, Hottest Fashion Warehouse or Capital Bank will not. Mr. I-Don't-Care-If-It-Was-Six-Years-Ago-When-You-Didn't-Know-Any-Better will call you at a time when you least expect or want him to (rightfully) demanding his money. If you've had any experience with collection agency representatives, you know they are a pain in the you-know-what. If you haven't, consider yourself blessed.

From a sports perspective, I challenge you to always play offense. Get good at it. For those of you who aren't sports smart, all this means is be proactive. Don't sit back passively waiting for your debtors to call. When you know you've got issues to handle, call or email your creditors first. If not, I can almost guarantee you will pay collection fees, interest, penalties, overdraft fees, and in some cases even attorney and court costs. If it gets to the point where the collector is making multiple attempts to reach you with no success, your payroll check could be garnished by the courts, or liens could be placed on your credit reports for overdue taxes. This could potentially stop you from getting a job or obtaining credit, as most creditors will not extend credit to you if you have a lien for fear that the lien will be attached to their asset, like your home, for example.

Hopefully, by the time you're done reading this, you'll have newfound boldness and will have no problem dealing directly with your finances. My prayer is that you'll feel confident in sharing what you've learned with others, even when they haven't asked you for your two cents. For the next few days, few weeks, or few hours (if you happen to be on a very long plane ride), let this book be your guide to understanding everyday questions about money. For the next twenty years, let it be your go-to financial reference. I've tried to make the info simple and relevant enough for the principles to endure the test of time.

Use the following steps as you begin to formalize and prioritize your expenses and debt within your budget.

Step 1 – Determine Your Status

Do you know what your status is? Are you currently avoiding blocked calls? Stop avoiding opening or regularly checking your mail. Your mail is stacking up like a dirty clothes pile. If your finances are in shambles I can almost guarantee you are stressed out, depressed, overeating, or not sleeping. If you are avoiding your mail or certain phone calls, this probably means that you've called the 800 number on the back of your debit or credit card right before you approached the cash register of your neighborhood Target. Cash uncertainty has probably led to you sweating in line, staring at the illuminated credit card keypad, while waiting for your transaction to be approved...or declined. We've all been there, making those calls in the car right before you enter the store, or worse yet, while in the store's bathroom, your cart of goodies right outside the door. When your card is declined, you make every excuse in the book, except for the right one: your finances weren't a priority. Or, in some cases, because you haven't kept proper records or communicated regularly with your spouse on your current situation, you make assumptions about what your bank or credit card balance should be.

I was in Target this past fall and a mother of three got in line with a cart full of items totaling close to $200. She and her small children had been in the store for several hours shopping through all the clearance items, then decided to get in line. I happened to be in line behind them and she got the total and attempted to foot the bill using 40 percent cash and putting 60 percent on her credit card. She tried seven different cards, and they were all declined. After watching the disappointment in those kids' faces and in the face of the mother for not being able to provide for the needs of her children, my wife and I gave each other "the look" and decided to pay it forward and pay the 60 percent.

I interpreted this situation as a sign of confirmation that I needed to write this book because people's finances are out of control. Some of you are taking the Kevin Hart approach. Your excuse goes a little something like, "The way that my bank account is set up, I gotta checking and a savings..." Seriously though, if these scenarios are currently taking place in your life, you are living with no financial margin. It is important that you live within your financial means, not above and beyond what you can realistically afford. When you do, you won't spend any unnecessary dollars on overdraft charges, payday loan fees, over-the-limit fees, etc.

In his financial series Money Matters, Dr. Vernon stated the simple goal as "more money than bills." So, whatever it takes to get to that point, within legal means, you should be willing to do. This will begin your journey to financial peace. It may mean downsizing your current living space, refinancing your home or car for a lower rate, working a second job, picking up more hours at your current job, acquiring additional education or training, and even cutting back on unnecessary spending. If you don't have money saved and are in serious debt, you shouldn't have cable, a luxurious cell phone like the iPhone 5s, or other items that are considered wants rather than needs. Sometimes, balance is created when you increase your income, while simultaneously decreasing your expenses. Maybe your car has put you over the edge, and you need to trade it in for something more affordable and easier to pay off. You should not drive a Mercedes Benz S550 and park it at your efficiency apartment; nor should you drive a Range Rover Sport while living in your parents' basement. Particularly, if you are not living in these places by choice, but because of your poor financial management skills.

Getting a pay increase or acquiring a new job is not an excuse to create new debt. Invest more in your retirement fund. Increase your savings account. Make sure your children are able to attend college debt free. Diversify your portfolio.

Step 2 – Know Your Income

Determine the total amount of your income. What is the total amount of wages received from your current employer during a pay period? If you're self-employed, how much are you earning on a weekly, bi-weekly, or monthly basis? Do you receive social security, unemployment, or a pension? Define the wages for your entire household, including your spouse. Determine the amount of all fixed income received on a monthly basis. Do not include child support, settlements, or tax refunds in your regular income; however, you can use this additional non-fixed income to assist with paying off debts quicker, investing in retirement, or increasing your savings account.

Step 3 – Calculate Your Fixed Living Expenses

Fixed living expenses are those that must be paid on a monthly basis, some of which will affect your monthly credit rating. These include: automobile and house notes, student loans any other loans you may have, and insurance costs. Other fixed expenses are utility payments, taxes, charitable donations, grocery costs, gasoline, clothing, entertainment, etc. The majority of these expenses are usually the same every month, rarely fluctuating. Fixed living expenses are needs, not wants.

Step 4 – Determine Your Discretionary Expenses

After establishing your fixed expenses, which should include your tithes, savings, and investments, determine where and how the rest of your income should be spent. Do you make unnecessary purchases on a continuous basis? To determine this, purchase a small notebook, no bigger than the size of your back pocket. The cost should be less than two bucks. Then, clean out your car armrest. For one full month, I want you to record every expense using the notebook. Write the date at the top of each page in order to track daily expenses. Write down every purchase from vending machines to the daily newspaper to packs of gum. For coffee lovers, every $3.00 cup of Starbucks should be recorded. You will be astonished when you see where your money is going on a monthly basis. Keep all of your receipts for the month in your armrest, including ATM receipts. At the end of the month, if you've kept detailed records, you will be able to calculate the figures from your notebook, in alignment with the receipts from your armrest. Calculate and total your discretionary expenses. Because it's been a habit to not keep track of where your money goes, I promise you, when you see the results, you'll be blown away.

Now that we have determined your fixed income, fixed expenses, and discretionary expenses, we are going to put a plan in place, the blueprint. If you follow it, this plan will ensure good stewardship. It doesn't matter how much money you make; what matters is how it's managed and spent. Remember our goal is more money than bills!

Step 5 – Create a Budget

In order to keep you focused, our next and final step is to draft a budget. Budgets are important even though, admittedly, they are challenging to create and even harder to follow. But allow me to encourage you: something that may sometimes seem like your worst enemy will in the future be your best friend financially.

It is critical that you provide honest answers to the following questions as you begin the process of creating your budget. The answers to these questions will help you establish your goals and priorities.

Do you pay your tithes? Just a little advice if you don't: Pay the 10 percent to ensure that the other ninety is blessed.

Do you have a savings account? Within your savings account, is there enough to cover three to six months of your total household bills and expenses? In other words, if you lost your job, would you be able to pay all of your household expenses for three to six months? Later in the book, I outline a 52 Week Savings Challenge. If you don't have three to six months of expenses saved, I encourage you to join me in the challenge.

Are you enrolled in your employer's 401k plan? If your current job doesn't have a 401k plan, are you saving for retirement?

Are you current on your bills?

Do you want to be an entrepreneur?

If you have children, do you have a college savings plan set up?

How much is your total debt? To whom and how much do you owe?

The answers to these questions will assist you in determining the amount to be allocated for savings and investments.

Let's Create the Budget

I won't assume everyone knows the definition of a budget. A budget is an estimate of income and expenditures for a set period of time. Usually, a budget describes a period in the future, not the past, in relation to economic terms. A budget is setting yourself up for where you'd like to be. It's difficult to set a budget if you haven't completed the aforementioned steps. Knowing the total amount of your income, monthly fixed and discretionary expenses and your future goals, are necessary steps to formulating an accurate household budget. Priorities are important when creating your budget. Be realistic with the time and resources needed to get goals accomplished, but aim high. For example, don't allocate $50 a month for gas if you drive twenty miles to your job five days a week. That's unrealistic. You're going to blow the budget in a week and get discouraged. However, if you spend $25 a week on in-app purchases from Candy Crush,

Scramble with Friends, or some other guilty pleasure, strike that from the budget immediately.

In order for this process to be successful, your entire household has to be aware of the budget and its intended goals. Everyone has to be willing to sacrifice in order to accomplish the goals. Problems are inevitable if your spouse doesn't buy in to the budget. There will be arguments and unnecessary discord if your family has not been a part of the budget-creating process and or participated in the steps implemented to arrive at the budget's intended purpose. While you can have personal financial goals, these and the household goals should be aligned as well. Distinguish between the two and make sure your family knows that the house goals are for the house, not just you individually, even if you are the one spearheading the initiative. Be sure to include them in a way that makes them feel like their contribution to the conversation is valuable.

Bring everyone to the table and discuss the findings from the prior steps. Ensure that you and your spouse are on one accord. Allow everyone to share their thoughts related to the process. This includes fears and misgivings. Once this is done, the budget can be created and managed in harmony, because everyone has voiced their feedback, experiences, and expectations.

Also, creating a budget isn't a one-shot-and-you're-done type of deal. You'll have to come back to it often; I would suggest weekly. You never know what might come up. There could be unexpected dentist bills or you may need to designate some funds for a birthday party for Junior, who'll be five next month. Having weekly meetings ensures that you and your family are always on the same page and allows you to call an audible midstream if you see one goal moving faster than another. The sooner you can get one accomplished, the better momentum you'll have to get the next one crossed off.

While you're in budget mode, eliminate using your ATM card and debit cards. Use only your savings account and go into the bank for any cash needs once a week. I know this is a tough one; we've become so reliant on those little plastic cards. But doing this will allow you to really get control of your finances because you'll see exactly what your cash position is on a daily basis. Most people never know their actual balance on a day-to-day basis. I call them "pending players." Something is always pending.

As a final point, it is always important that everyone understands how the budget will affect them presently, as well as in the future. The positive effects will be less stress, more family vacations in the future, more savings/margin, and the ability to purchase a home. When all expenses are accounted for, try to work toward living on one income.

As you create your budget, do it with the recommended percentages below in mind. This will ensure you are paying your tithes, paying yourself, in addition to paying towards your future, while maintaining good stewardship over your fixed expenses. The discretionary fund will be the margin you need for any unforeseen expenditures.

Let's begin with baby steps, a 30 Day Budget Challenge. Follow through on the five steps within thirty days. Pastor Donald Donaldson of Rose Hill Church in Baton Rouge, New Orleans says, "Habits change circumstances." So, let's get started!

Recommended Budget Breakdown (Financially Unstable):

1. Tithes – 10 percent

2. Savings – 5 percent

3. Investments (College, Retirement) – 5 percent

4. Fixed Expenses – 80 percent (Inclusive of debt cancellation)

Example: If your monthly income is $2000.00 per month (net), your budget would look like this:

1. Tithes - $200.00

2. Savings (rainy day and long-term) - $100.00

3. Investments - $100.00

4. Fixed expenses - $1600.00

5. Discretionary expenses/margin - $0.00

Budget Breakdown (Financially Stable):

1. Tithes – 10 percent

2. Savings (rainy day and long-term) – 10 percent

3. Investments (college, retirement) – 10 percent

4. Fixed expenses – 65 percent

5. Rainy day/discretionary – 5 percent

Example: If your monthly income is $2000.00 per month (net), your budget would look like this:

1. Tithes - $200.00

2. Savings - $200.00

3. Investments - $200.00

4. Fixed expenses - $1300.00

5. Discretionary expenses/margin - $100.00

Note: Your rainy day savings is the money earmarked for immediate but unexpected necessities, such as vehicle repair. Your long-term savings is your worst-case scenario option (job loss), but could also be used for a lofty but worthy goal, like the down payment for your first home. Long-term funds are not spent until your rainy day fund is depleted.

Sample Personal Budget

Download a free personal budget from one of the below mentioned sites. For your convenience you can download the app or utilize your desktop. Utilize it to track spending and expenses.

www.budgetpulse.com

www.budgettracker.com

www.quickbooksonline.com

www.mint.com

You can also use software like Microsoft Money or Quicken. If you're an old school player who prefers to do your business the old-fashioned way, a handy dandy notebook will work (almost) just as well.

Once you have created your budget, purchase a large poster board. On the poster board, list your most important financial goals. Then, print a copy of your budget and attach it to the poster board. Hang the poster board in an area where your entire family can view it. This will serve as a daily reminder of your financial goals. As you pay off debt or purchase something you've been saving for, make adjustments to the budget. Cross out the goals you've met to help keep the positive energy flowing and create an optimistic attitude throughout your household. Repeat the same steps till you've met the next goal.

The process will be arduous, but it can be done! In many instances, not only will you be working to change your mindset, but the financial mindset of your entire family.

Implement the snowball approach Dave Ramsey discusses in his book, *The Total Money Makeover*. Pay your lowest bills first. Once those are paid, use the money you were using to pay the lowest bills towards the next set of bills. Continue this process until all of your debt is eliminated. The reason you start with the lowest bills is to create momentum, like a snowball rolling down a hill. It starts off small, then it becomes bigger as it rolls. You can eliminate $300 a lot quicker than $3000. The sense of accomplishment you'll feel eliminating your debt will fuel your need to meet all of your financial goals.

After you begin the budget process, once a month, take one of your weekly family financial budget meetings to evaluate your overall progress. If you're single, meet with yourself. The more disciplined you get, the less frequently you will need to meet. During your monthly meeting, make any necessary adjustments.

Rome wasn't built in a day. It will take several months to get the process moving forward (estimate three to four months). It will take dedication and discipline to see true results. Once you get through the first year, budgeting will become a habit. If you have children, this will become a great teaching tool that they will one day implement in their own households. You can be proud of yourself for taking responsibility for your finances and setting your children up to be financially responsible as well.

2

READ THE REPORT

———

Breaking Down Your Credit Report

The Lord your God will bless you as he has promised. You will lend money to many nations, but will never need to borrow. You will rule many nations, but they will not rule over you. (Deuteronomy 15:6 NLT)

You've probably read other authors who discuss the power of using cash versus borrowing on credit. The author advises you to spend cash on all purchases, stressing the importance of avoiding debt. I agree that most items should be paid for with cash (clothing, electronics, furniture, etc.). Keep in mind, though, the average person can't afford to purchase their home or car with cash. If you own a business or aspire to be an entrepreneur, credit is necessary to stabilize and assist with growing your business, unless you have private investors, who in most cases may want equity or a percentage of your sales. I refer to this type of debt as understandable debt. I believe when you obtain these debts, you should do everything in your power to remain a good steward, eliminating the debts as quickly as possible.

So, we need to discuss what your credit report entails and answer any questions you may have. If you decide to enter into a financial transaction that requires you to obtain credit, within minutes of meeting you the lender or salesperson will know your entire credit history. I want to ensure you have no surprises or are not taken advantage of. We will discuss in this chapter that just spending thirty to ninety days, in some cases, will be sufficient time to make certain repairs to your credit report.

Financial institutions are in business to make money, not friends. So, do business and keep the emotions to yourself. Take control and pay your debt on your terms. Be smart and eliminate interest rapidly. Don't be too happy when you're approved for a loan. No, it is not always an occasion to celebrate, because sometimes it's a Band-Aid to a current situation. Recognize what the costs are, and strategize how to best use the bank's money to your benefit. This is where the education provided within this book and online will help you negotiate the best interest rate, terms and product costs. Also, shameless plug, follow me @laresepurnell on Twitter and Instagram where I will share random financial facts.

The saying goes, "There's a fool born every day." So, don't ever pay the sticker price on pretty much anything; the seller always has wiggle room. Fall in love with the deal not the item, and like I just mentioned, keep emotions to yourself. Once the deal is closed look for strategies to eliminate the debt. You have to do your homework. The lender is only going to share certain strategies to help you eliminate their loan. If you're purchasing a home or vehicle see the example below:

Cost Saving Scenario:

Imagine you are purchasing a home for $289,406. You want to eliminate the debt quicker and at a lower cost. See the example for how to make this happen. (Provided by Nationwide Biweekly Administration)

	Sample Comparison: (figures are estimates) Payment may be lower or higher.		
	Payment $	**Years to Pay**	**Interest Savings**
Monthly:	$2,158	23.9	$54,987
Bi-Weekly:	$1,079	23.9	$54,987
Weekly:	$540	23.9	$56,434

Weekly & Bi-Weekly Debits: (sample comparison)

1. Smaller debit amount. ($540 weekly or $1,079 bi-weekly)

2. Can be set up to match your pay schedule.

3. Budgeting is easier because a smaller amount can be taken from each pay period.

By employing this method and adding a little more to your payments, those additional payments will be added directly to your principal, referred to as principal only payments. Whenever you decide to make additional payments towards the loan, make sure you indicate that you want those payments to go toward the principal only, not the interest. Most institutions will have payment slips for principal only payments. Also, let your mortgage lender know that these are the terms under which you would like to process future payments and in most cases, they will assist you with making sure this takes place.

Every institution processes this method differently. When you make these payments, be sure to verify that your principal has been reduced, and that the company has not paid you ahead and deducted interest. (If you're not a math wizard, or if you're too busy to try to figure out these numbers by hand, check out www.bankrate.com for all sorts of helpful calculators to help you determine how much money you're spending or saving). If you're obsessive-compulsive and you want to be totally sure the extra money you send is being applied appropriately, send two checks and clearly mark them "principal" and "interest." You will save money in interest, while decreasing the number of years of the loan. At the same time, as it relates to your mortgage, your home's equity will increase.

Make use of this same method on all loans and/or credit cards. Never pay minimum payments! When you do, all you're paying are fees and interest. Some credit statements display your monthly history based on your current balance. If you made monthly minimum payments, they display only how long it would take to pay the balance. So don't take three years to pay three hundred dollars back. The key is to use their money for convenience purposes. Only borrow what you can afford to pay back.

Credit Score

A credit score is a number assigned to a person that indicates to lenders their capacity to repay a loan, or to put it another way, an analysis of a person's creditworthiness. This score typically ranges from 300-850 with numbers at the higher end indicating a person is less of a credit risk.

The gold standard for credit scores is FICO, which has been around for about twenty years. Ninety of the top one hundred largest U.S. financial institutions use the FICO Score to make consumer credit decisions. However, each of the three credit bureaus has their own scoring systems and designations. Experian's is the PLUS score, Equifax's is Score Power, and TransUnion, who wasn't as creative, just calls theirs Credit Score. There is also the Vantage Score, introduced in 2006 to compete with FICO, which is collectively owned by all three of the credit bureaus. Let me confuse you even more: You actually have three FICO scores, one at each of the three bureaus and they each have different names, and yes, these are different from the proprietary scores the bureaus have come up with. For more information, visit www.myfico.com.

Why all these scoring models? Simply because different lenders evaluate different things about you to determine whether or not they want to loan you money. This is why it is a good idea to obtain all three of your credit reports. You may be surprised to find that each report contains different information about you. If you really want to know what lenders or potential employers can see, you need to get all three.

So what's a good credit score? Well, again, the answer is not as straightforward as it might seem, but in general, here's what experts say:

760-850: Excellent

700-759: Very Good

660-699: Good

620-659: Fair

619 or less: Bad

Credit Reporting Agency	FICO Score
Equifax	BEACON® Score
Experian	Experian/FICO Risk Model
TransUnion	FICO® Risk Score, Classic

If you fall in the "bad" range, don't fret too much. There are things you can do to improve your score. And although 619 or less is considered poor by many scoring standards, a person can get approved for an FHA mortgage loan with a score of 580. Of course, that person would most likely be burdened with a higher interest rate than a person with a score of 740, but the fact is, a lender will examine various aspects of your credit portfolio to determine whether or not to extend you credit and at what rate.

Rather than getting caught up in which of the myriad credit scores you should be paying attention to: (1) pay your bills on time; (2) don't use more than 30 percent of your credit limit; (3) don't borrow more money than you can afford to pay back; and (4) use the tools available to you (many of them free) to monitor your credit regularly for fraudulent activity.

Maintaining good credit is crucial if you are to remain a good steward over your finances. Poor credit gives financial institutions the advantage when you're applying for a loan. Your name does mean something, so manage it. When purchasing a car or a home, (one of) your credit scores will determine your cost. Based on the score they use, the lender will determine your interest rate and the length of time (term) you have to pay the loan back, in addition to the monthly cost of the item you're acquiring.

Build a strong credit score. Yes, you can build or even repair your credit score. Bear in mind, you're not just building a strong score to acquire things in life. Nowadays, potential employers evaluate your credit history as a way to judge your character and discipline. Thus, it is vital to obtain your credit score, even if you're not purchasing a car or home. The steps I recommend to repair or build a new credit score are:

1. Set up all items that are on your credit report for automatic deduction (payments taken right from your bank account) to ensure you make timely payments

2. Keep your debt-utilization ratio under 30 percent of your available credit balance. For example, if you have a Target card with available credit of $1000, your balance shouldn't exceed $300.

3. Review your credit report and dispute any errors. I have dealt with clients with debts on their reports that actually belonged to their parents.

4. Minimize the amount of times you apply for new credit, especially if you don't need it.

5. Monitor your credit to ensure you eliminate the chance of identity theft; consider putting a security freeze on credit reports.

6. Sign up for credit monitoring, like www.creditkarma.com, www.quizzle.com www.creditsesame.com to be aware of your credit status.

7. Don't let disputes and bills go to collections; negotiate with vendors.

8. Get two major credit cards. Most financial institutions want you to have at least two lines of credit to approve you for a vehicle or mortgage loan.

9. Consolidate debt on your report so that you don't show multiple credit cards with high utilization percentages.

10. Be careful when you close your credit cards. This affects your credit history and total available credit on your report.

11. Catch up on any missed payments; bring past-due accounts to current status.

12. Negotiate all collection accounts. Pay them off and follow up to ensure they show as paid and closed on your report.

13. Pay any liens, get a receipt for your records, and make sure it shows released on your report.

Having no credit, in some cases, is just as damaging as having bad credit. I advise you to apply for at least two credit cards. Use them responsibly for expenses like gas, groceries, and other day-to-day purchases. Make sure you make your payments on time, and if possible, pay off the full balance every month. If you don't pay it off in full, make sure that the balance never exceeds 30 percent of the credit limit.

Before making any of the major purchases we've previously discussed, do your research. When purchasing a vehicle, go in knowing your credit score, as well as the value of the vehicle you are purchasing and/or trading in. Visit Kelley's Blue Book (KBB) at www.kbb.com and www.edmunds.com. These sites will provide you with information like:

1. What you should pay for a new car

2. What you should pay for a used car

3. What your current car is worth

4. What car is right for you

KBB will also assist with:

1. Calculating payments

2. Shared vehicle history

3. Rebates and incentives

4. Comparing cars

Being an educated consumer will help limit unwanted surprises presented by salespeople or finance representatives. When you can converse knowledgeably about making large purchases or attempting to acquire financing, your confidence tells the salesperson that you are prepared, forcing them to put the best deal on the table.

One of my closest friends, Stacy Collins, always says, "Fall in love with the deal, not the item you're purchasing." Sometimes you have to be willing to walk away. As a matter-of-fact, when you're negotiating, always be willing to walk away. If the deal is not right for you, then wait until it is or find someone else to negotiate with. Shop around and do your due diligence. Search your local newspaper and popular sites for buying cars like www.autotrader.com and www.cars.com before you set foot on anyone's showroom floor.

Now, let's inspect your credit report. When is the last time you saw a copy of your credit report? Have you ever looked at your credit report? If so, do you understand what you're reading? Do you know what's on it and if it's correct? Together, let's figure out what companies are looking for when making the decision to grant a loan approval.

Who cares about your credit scores?

- Lenders, to determine approval for loans or credit cards, along with the interest rates and terms

- Insurers, in order to set premiums

- Cell phone companies, to determine qualification for contracts

- Utility companies, for the purpose of deposits

- Landlords, in order to grant approvals for moving into their properties

- Employers, to decide on new employment positions

Five C's Lenders Use When Extending Credit:

According to Investopedia, The Five C's approach to evaluating a borrower incorporates both qualitative and quantitative measures. The first factor of consideration is **character**, which refers to a borrower's reputation. The second is **capacity**, which measures a borrower's ability to repay a loan by comparing income against recurring debts. The lender will consider any **capital**—the third factor—that the borrower puts toward a potential investment, because a large contribution by the borrower will lessen the chance of default. The fourth factor is **collateral**, such as property or large assets, which helps to secure the loan. Finally, the **conditions** of the loan, such as the interest rate and amount of principal, will influence the lender's desire to finance the borrower.

Reasons You Can Receive a Free Credit Report

You can obtain a free report once a year from www.annualcreditreport.com, although, this does NOT give you your credit score.

- If you are turned down for credit, employment, or insurance within a sixty day period (You must send written proof of your denials to the credit bureaus when requesting your free report)

- If you were charged higher rates, fees, or deposits based on a credit report issued by a credit bureau

- If you certify in writing that you are unemployed and plan to seek employment within sixty days

- If you are a recipient of public assistance

- If you are a victim of fraud

Who are the Credit Reporting Agencies?

The three national credit agencies may be contacted directly. See the following:

- Equifax – Report is mailed within forty-eight hours

- TransUnion – Receive within six to eight business days

- Experian – Receive within eight to ten business days

Caution: If the letter you send to the credit agency regarding your denial is received after the sixty-day period, you may have to pay for the report. It would be advantageous to mention in your letter the date that you actually requested the report. If you called and requested the credit report, indicate the date you made the call. Your written request should contain proof of your identity and current address, usually your driver's license, state ID, or a copy of your utility bill.

Free Credit Report Options:

To ensure a strong credit score is maintained, you must view your credit report and score quarterly. Visit www.creditkarma.com, www.quizzle.com, and www.creditsesame.com, sign up for a free membership, check your credit report, and receive access to your score. Credit Karma updates your score on a weekly basis. You will have the ability to receive daily alerts indicating changes on your

Equifax	TransUnion	Experian
www.equifax.com	www.transunion.com	www.experian.com
P.O. Box 740241	P.O. Box 1000	P.O. Box 2002
Atlanta, GA 30374	Chester, PA 19022	Allen, TX 75013
800-685-1111	800-888-4213	1-888-397-3742

credit report. This will allow you to catch any fraudulent activity and inquiries (companies viewing your report) on a more frequent basis.

Credit Karma will also provide you with a Vantage, Auto Insurance, and Home Insurance Score. The report and score provided on this site will be retrieved from TransUnion only.

If you would like to review all three credit scores and reports on a monthly basis, sign up at www.creditreport.com. Initially, the cost will be one dollar for a seven-day trial. Then you will pay $24.95 per month to receive a new credit report and score from all three credit bureaus.

Credit Report Request Letter

This letter should be used to obtain a free credit report based on credit denial. If you have been denied credit based on the information in your credit file within the last sixty days, you are entitled to a free copy of your credit report from that credit bureau.

Sample Letter #1

(Date)

Equifax Information Service Center
P.O. Box 105873
Atlanta, GA 30348

Experian, Inc.
P.O. Box 2002
Allen, TX 75013

TransUnion Corporation
Consumer Disclosure Center
P.O. Box 1000
Chester, PA 19022

RE: My Credit Report

To whom it may concern,

In accordance with the Federal Fair Credit Reporting Act (FCRA), I wish to request a free copy of my credit report to ensure that it is correct. My details are:

Name:

Social Security Number:

Birth Date:

Current Employer:

Previous Employer:

Years I have lived at my current address:

Previous addresses during the last five years:

Spouse's Name:

Sincerely,

(Your Name)
(Address - City, State and ZIP Code)
(Your phone number)

Sample Letter #2

*****Insert Bureau Address Here*****

RE: Request for Deletions of Inaccurate Credit Information

Name:

Current Address:

Social Security Number:

Date of Birth:

To whom it may concern:

I have received a copy of my credit report and find the following items to be in error. Attached is a copy of my credit report.

Item and Account Number:

Nature of Dispute:

Item and Account Number:

Nature of Dispute:

Item and Account Number:

Nature of Dispute:

By the provisions of Section 611 of the Fair Credit and Reporting Act of 1970, I demand these items be deleted from all current and future credit reports. Please forward the names of any individuals and/or organizations you contacted so I may follow up with them directly. I shall assume that thirty days constitutes a "reasonable time" for re-verification of these entries. Through our interpretation of Section 611(a), it is understood that the failure to re-verify these items within thirty days constitutes a reason to promptly drop the information from the credit report.

Pursuant to Section 611(d) of The Fair Credit and Reporting Act, please send notification that these items have been deleted. Please send an updated credit report to my address that is listed above. The provisions of section 612 state that there is no charge for this notification.

Respectfully,

(Your Signature)

Sample Credit Report

```
                          SAMPLE CREDIT REPORT
┌──────────────────────────────────────────────────────────────────┐
│                          CREDIT REPORT                             │
└──────────────────────────────────────────────────────────────────┘

  1 DUNCAN,ELIZABETH*2 9923,,WOODBINE,,CHICAGO,IL,60693*3 10,N,CAMINO,,OAKLAND
  ,CA,94583*5 001-01-0418**

                        TRANS UNION CREDIT REPORT

○ <FOR>          <SUB NAME>       <MKT SUB>  <INFILE>   <DATE>      <TIME>
  (I) D248       ABC DEPT STORE   06 CH      4/74       12/15/94    09:36CT

  <SUBJECT>                                  <SSN>          <BIRTH DATE>
○ DUNCAN, ELIZABETH                          001-01-0418    2/53
  <ALSO KNOWN AS>                                           <TELEPHONE>
  COOK, ELIZABETH                                           555-4212

  <CURRENT ADDRESS>                                         <DATE RPTD>
  9932 WOODBINE, #9B CHICAGO IL. 60693                      11/93
  <FORMER ADDRESS>
  10 N. CAMINO, OAKLAND CA. 94583                           2/92
                                   <POSITION>
  <CURRENT EMPLOYER AND ADDRESS>   <INCOME> <VERF> <RPTD> <HIRE>
  MARRIOTT HOTELS                  CONCIERGE
  8638 GRAND, ANYTOWN IL.          32500Y  11/94  11/94  11/91
  ------------------------------------------------------------------
  S P E C I A L   M E S S A G E S
○ ***TRANS-ALERT: INPUT ADDRESS DOES NOT MATCH FILE ADDRESS***
○ ***HAWK-ALERT: VERIFY INPUT...
       - CURRENT ADDRESS IS COMMERCIAL
  ------------------------------------------------------------------
  M O D E L   P R O F I L E       ○ * * * A L E R T * * *
○ ***NEW DELPHI ALERT: SCORE○+775: 26, 03, 06, 25 ***
  ------------------------------------------------------------------
  C R E D I T   S U M M A R Y   * * *   T O T A L  F I L E  H I S T O R Y
○ PR=1○COL=1○NEG=1○HSTNEG-1-6 ○ TRD=2○RVL=1○INST=1○MTG=0○OPN=0○INQ=2
           ○HIGH CRED○CRED LIM○BALANCE○PAST DUE○MNTHLY PAY AVAILABLE
  REVOLVING:   $500     $1000    $100     $       $20      ○90%
  INSTALLMENT: $16.0K   $        $12.4K   $1974   $282
○ TOTALS:     $16.5K   $1000    $12.5K   $1974   $302
  ------------------------------------------------------------------
○P U B L I C   R E C O R D S
  SOURCE   DATE    LIAB      ECOA         ASSETS    DOCKET#
  TYPE                       COURT LOC              PLAINTIFF/ATTORNEY
  Z 4932059 6/94R $13.0K    C            $0         94938521
  CIVIL JUDGMENT             CHICAGO, IL             R. SMITH/D. WINSLOW
  ------------------------------------------------------------------
○C O L L E C T I O N S
  SUBNAME       SUBCODE  ECOA OPENED  CLOSED  $PLACED  CREDITOR       MOP
  ACCOUNT#               VERIFIED             BALANCE  REMARKS
  ADVANCED COL. Y 999C004 I  1/94   1/94F  $2500   ABC BANK          O9P
  12345                      12/94A         $1000   MAKING PAYMENTS
  ------------------------------------------------------------------
  T R A D E S
○ SUBNAME    ○SUBCODE ○OPENED○HIGHCRED  TERMS   ○MAXDELQ○PAYPAT 1-12 MOP
○ ACCOUNT#            ○VERFIED○CREDLIM ○PASTDUE ○AMT-MOP○PAYPAT 13-24
○ ECOA_COLLATRL/LOANTYPE CLSD/PD BALANCE○REMARKS        ○MO 30/60/90

  AMERICAN BK  B 6661001  5/93   $16.0K  60M282   12/94  543323211111 10S
  9876543210             12/94A          $1974    $1974 05 1111111
  I    NISSAN MAXIMA             $12.4K  *CONTACT SUBSCRIBER  19V 2/ 3/ 2

  FILENE$        D 3847002  4/90  $500    MIN20          111111111111 R01
  2212345678               12/94A $1000                  111111111111
  C    /CREDIT CARD              $100                    48V 0/ 0/ 0
  ------------------------------------------------------------------
○I N Q U I R I E S
  DATE       SUBCODE   SUBNAME             DATE     SUBCODE   SUBNAME
  12/15/94   DCH248    ABC DEPT STORE :    11/7/94  BPM9999   TEST BANK
  ------------------------------------------------------------------
○E N D   O F   C R E D I T   R E P O R T  -  S E R V I C E D   B Y :
  TRANS UNION CORPORATION                                810-524-2222
  PO BOX 390, SPRINGFIELD, PA. 19064
```

43

Your Credit Report

Please address all future
correspondence to:
Credit Reporting Agency
Business Address
City, State 00000

Personal Identification

This is all the information that uniquely identifies you from another person who may have the same name.

PERSONAL IDENTIFICATION INFORMATION

Your Name
123 Current Address
City, State 00000

SSN #: 123-45-6789
Date of Birth: July 1, 1958
Telephone Number: (555) 555-5555

EMPLOYMENT DATE REPORTED

Employer Name: Employer 1
Date Reported: 06/2004

Position: Job/Occupation
Hired: 04/2004

Public Records

These listings show any legal information that may affect your credit ranking.

PUBLIC RECORD INFORMATION

Lien Filed 03/93; Fulton CTY; Case or Other ID Number-32114; Amount-$26,667
Class-State; Released 07/93; Verified 07/93

Bankruptcy Filed 12/92; Northern District Ct; Case or Other ID Number-673HC12;
Liabilities-$15,787; Personal; Individual; Discharged; Assets-$780

Satisfied Judgment Filed 07/94; Fulton CTY; Case or Other ID Number-898872; Defendant-
Consumer; Amount-$8,984; Plaintiff-ABC Real Estate; Satisfied 03/95; Verified 05/95

Collections

Any collection agencies assigned to recover outstanding debts will be listed here.

COLLECTION AGENCY ACCOUNT INFORMATION

Pro Coll (800)XXX-XXXX
Collection Reported 05/07; Assigned 09/04 to Pro Coll (800)XXX-XXXX Client-ABC
Hospital; Amount-$978; Unpaid; Balance $978; Date of Last Activity 09/04; Individual
Account; Account Number 797652JC

Credit Accounts

Installment loan accounts will be listed here, such as school loans, auto loans and mortgages. Revolving credit amounts will also be listed. These may include credit cards, store cards and gas cards. This gives credit issuers information on payment history.

CREDIT ACCOUNT INFORMATION

COMPANY NAME	ACCOUNT NUMBER	WHOSE ACCT.	DATE OPENED	MONTHS REVIEWED	DATE OF LAST ACTIVITY	HIGH CREDIT	TERMS	BALANCE	PAST DUE	STATUS	DATE REPORTED
Department St.	32514	J	10/06	36	9/06	$950	X	$0	X	R1	10/06
Bank	1004735	A	11/96	24	5/06	$750	X	$0	X	I1	4/06
Oil Company	541125	A	6/06	12	3/06	$500	X	$0	X	O1	4/06
Auto Finance	529778	I	5/95	48	12/07	$1100	$50	$300	$200	I5	4/06

Previous Payment History: 3 Times 30 days late; 4 Times 60 days late; 2 Times 90+ days late
Previous Status: 01/08 - I2; 02/08 - I3; 03/08 - I4

COMPANIES THAT REQUESTED YOUR CREDIT FILE

09/06/08	Equifax-Disclosure	08/27/08	Department Store
07/29/08	PRM Bankcard	07/03/08	AM Bankcard
04/10/08	AR Department Store	12/31/07	Equifax-Disclosure ACIS 123456789

Requested Credit Files

This is a list of any companies who have requested information on your credit history. On this example Equifax may have requested information in response to a credit application.

Components of a Credit Report:

Make sure you review these areas at least every three months for accuracy.

1. **Personal information** including your name, address, and place of employment is used to identify you. Previous addresses and places of employment might also be included.

It's not uncommon to have variations or misspellings of your name. Most credit reporting agencies leave these variations to maintain the link between your identity and the credit information. Having different variations of your name and old addresses won't hurt your credit score as long as it's actually your information. Make sure personal information is identifying you and not someone else.

Sample Credit Report
Date of Report: 12/15/1999

Consumer Info

Name	Jane Doe
Also Known As	
Address(es)	123 Apple Lane Anywhere, OH 12345 456 Dove Street Flying High, CA 55443
Current Employer	Pretend Manufacturing
Previous Employer(s)	Not Reported

2. **The credit summary** section of your credit report summarizes information about the different types of accounts you have. This section lists the total number, balance, number current, and number of delinquent accounts. It will include the following account types:

- Real estate accounts, any mortgages present

- Revolving accounts, like credit cards and lines of credit

- Installment accounts, like loans

- Other accounts

- Collection accounts

Your credit summary will also summarize the number of accounts you have open, closed, in public records, and the number of inquiries made against your credit within the past two years.

Credit Summary

Revolving Accounts	
Count	4
Balance	5678
Current	3
Delinquent	1
Other	
Total Accounts	
Count	6
Balance	127,428
Current	5
Delinquent	1
Other	
Accounts Summary	
Open	6
Closed	0
Public Records	0
Inquiries (Prev 2 Yrs)	4

3. **The account history** section of your credit report contains the bulk of the information. This section includes each of your credit accounts and details about your payment history. Your account history will be very detailed, but it's important that you read

through it entirely, to ensure the information is being reported accurately.

Each account will contain several pieces of information.

- **Creditor name** of the institution reporting the information.

- **Account number** associated with the account. The account number may be scrambled or shortened for privacy purposes.

- **Account Type**, i.e. revolving account, education loan, auto loan.

- **Responsibility**, which indicates whether you have individual, joint, or authorized user responsibility for the account.

- **Monthly payment** is the minimum amount you are required to pay on the account each month.

- **Date opened** is the month and year the account was established.

- **Date reported** is the last date the creditor updated the account information with the credit bureau.

- **Balance** is the amount owed on the account at the time data was reported.

- **Credit limit or loan amount**

- **High balance or high credit** is the highest amount ever charged on the credit card. For installment loans, high credit is the original loan amount.

- **Past due** is the amount past due at the time the data was reported.

- **Remarks** are comments made by the creditor about your account.

- **Payment status** indicates the status of the account, i.e. current, past due, charge-off. Even if your account is current, it might contain information about previous delinquencies.

- **Payment history** indicates your monthly payment status since the time the account was established.

- **Collection accounts** may appear as part of the account history or in a separate section. Where it appears depends on the company providing your credit report.

Account History

Creditor Name	
Account Number	1234-xxxx-xxxx-xxxx
Account Type	Revolving
Responsibility	Individual
Monthly Payment	$55
Date Opened	9/1998
Date Reported	12/1999
Balance	$2750
Credit Limit	$5000
High Balance	$3500
Past Due	$0
Remarks	Current, was 90 days past due
Payment Status	Current

Payment History											
Year One											
1998>											
1	2	3	4	5	6	7	8	9	10	11	12
Ok	Ok	Ok	Ok	Ok	30	Ok	Ok	Ok	Ok	30	60

4. **Public records** include information like bankruptcies, judgments, tax liens, state, and county court records. In some states overdue child support is also included. Depending on the type of account, a public record can remain on your credit report between seven and ten years. Only severe financial blunders appear in this section, not criminal arrests or convictions. Public records can severely damage your credit, so it's best to keep this section clear.

Public Records

Bankruptcy	
Type	Chapter 7 Bankruptcy
Status	Discharged
Date Filed	3/25/1996
Reference Number	B350578609
Closing Date	5/25/1996
Court	County
Liability	65,700
Exempt Amount	0
Asset Amount	0
Remarks	

5. **Credit inquiries** list all parties who have accessed your credit report within the past two years. While your version of the credit report lists several credit inquiries, not all of these appear on the lender or creditor versions. Only "hard" inquiries are shown to lenders. These are inquiries made when a lender checks your credit report to approve your credit application. Your version will also include "soft" inquiries consisting of inquiries made by lenders for promotional purposes.

Credit Inquiries

Creditor	Date of Inquiry
Bank of USA	9/7/1999
Orange Mortgages	8/15/1998

3

LET'S SETTLE THE SCORE

———

Understanding your Credit Score

It is better that you should not vow than that you should vow and not pay. (Ecclesiastes 5:5 NASB)

Every athlete and spectator alike knows that in sports, you have to keep your eye on the score. The goal of any team or player is to score as many points as possible and hope that it's enough to beat their opponent. The score determines whether you win or lose.

As a consumer, your credit score is just as important to you as the game score is to the competitor. It's you versus the creditor, and you have to know what your score is, how to maintain it, and even more important than simply maintaining it, you have to know what to do to consistently increase it. The higher your score the better chances you have of winning at the consumerism contest. A high score allows you to negotiate better rates and stand firm in your position. A great score gives you great leverage, and allows you to play offensive when you enter the creditor's playing field. It allows you to bring less cash to the table and take advantage of the best score possible.

In this chapter, I'll discuss the credit score range and what your credit score is comprised of. You must pull all three reports and scores to get an accurate picture of your credit portfolio. Different agencies report different aspects of your credit history and are provided different information based on the lender; these things allow your score to vary. If your reports have different information, that is, a particular bureau doesn't report a credit account or adds false information to your credit file, it will affect the score provided by that individual bureau. The bureaus use this information to evaluate your credit worthiness, but remember, your past doesn't dictate your future. If you've had some credit challenges in the past, this is a new season. There are some choices you can make immediately that will over time have a cumulative, favorable impact on your score.

Speaking of which, when was the last time you checked your score? If the answer is "never" or "it's been a while," then today is a mighty fine day to do so. Visit www.myfico.com, www.annualcreditreport.com, or www.creditreport.com to receive a free trial period to review your scores (usually at least seven days, after which you will be billed monthly). Also, if you have been denied credit or your interest rate has increased on a current debt then you are entitled to a free score.

As we discussed in the prior chapter, federal law requires each of the three nationwide consumer credit reporting companies—Equifax, Experian, and TransUnion—to give you a free credit report every twelve months if you ask for it. They also make it easy to accomplish many credit-related tasks right from your computer. However, they are not required to provide your score to you at no cost.

People confuse the terms credit report and credit score, Investopedia defines credit score as a statistically derived numeric expression of a person's creditworthiness that is used by lenders to assess the likelihood that a person will repay his or her debts. A credit score is based on, among other things, a person's past credit history. It is a number between 300 and 850; the higher the number, the more creditworthy the person is deemed to be. A credit score is utilized by creditors to determine if they will extend credit.

There are a multitude of credit-scoring models in existence, but there's one that dominates the market: the FICO credit score. FICO is an acronym for the Fair Isaac Corporation. According to www.myfico.com, the consumer website for the FICO score developer, "Ninety percent of all financial institutions in the U.S. employ FICO scores in their decision-making process."

Example of the various credit scoring methods:

FICO score range: 300 – 850
FICO NextGen Score Range: 150–950
Vantage Score Range: 501 – 990
Equifax Credit Score Range: 280 – 850
Experian PLUS Score Range: 330 – 830

Experian's National Equivalency Score range: 360 – 840
Trans Risk New Account Score range: 300 – 850

The FICO credit score, calculated by the Fair Isaac Corporation, represents the most widely used credit scoring system. It parses data from the three major credit bureaus, breaking the numbers down into five main components. Each of the five components is weighted according to time-tested methods of consumer payment behavior, in addition to the likelihood that credit accounts will be paid in full. The FICO scale comprises numbers ranging from 300 to 850 as indicators of your credit score.

Credit Score Rating Chart	
Credit Score	**Description**
760 - 849	Excellent score. The lender will offer you their best interest rate.
700 - 759	Great score. There won't be any trouble in getting a loan at good interest rate.
660 - 699	Good score. There won't be any problem in getting a loan at good interest rate.
620 - 659	Fair score. You may qualify for the loan but not at good interest rates.
580 - 619	Poor score. You may qualify but the interest rates will be very high.
500 - 579	Very poor score. It's doubtful that you may qualify for the loan, and if you qualify, the interest rates will be extremely high.

A consumer has three FICO scores. There is a FICO score for each credit report provided by the three major credit bureaus: Equifax, Experian, and TransUnion. As discussed earlier in the chapter all three scores vary based on the information displayed by the three credit bureaus, so be sure to evaluate your reports for accurate information.

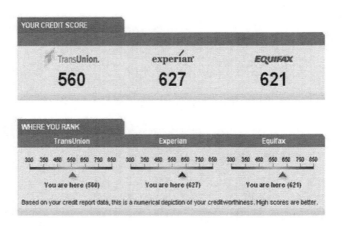

This is an example of pulling three credit scores and all of them being different. Again, it is very important that you continue to understand that financial institutions and creditors are in business to make money, not friends. Work hard to build a great score. The examples below show you how your credit score affects the interest rate you are given, what your payment amount will be, and the interest paid over the life of the loan.

The more money you can save based on receiving a lower interest rate the more dollars you can pay towards the principal of the debt to eliminate it quicker and at a lower cost. I know you have heard the phrase "Use the bank's money." That's essentially what you're doing when you use credit. You're using the bank's money to acquire goods and services as opposed to using your own. There is nothing wrong with that when you have a plan to pay the bank their money back and eliminate the debt. Keep in mind, however, there is a cost to use someone else's money—your interest rate—hence the reason you want to maintain a high credit score and pay off the debt as quickly as possible.

FICO Score	APR	Monthly Payments	Total Interest Paid
760-850	3.124%	$1,285	$162,587
700-759	3.346%	1,321	175,732
680-699	3.523%	1,351	186,356
660-679	3.737%	1,387	199,368
640-659	4.167%	1,461	226,060
620-639	4.713%	1,558	260,973

Source: MyFICO.com.

Notice that in this example, over the life of the loan, a person in the bottom credit score range will pay almost $3,276 more yearly than the person in the top range! I know you could use that money to save or invest.

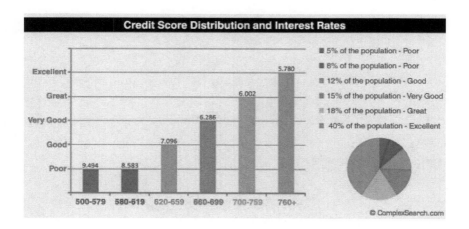

How does a creditor or lender perceive a score?

- Excellent credit score: 760 and Up

I want everyone to shoot for this range. Take power over your credit situation. If your score is in this range it will position you to receive the best possible interest rates when applying for credit. At this point you will be able to take advantage of those car payment deals that are posted in the weekly newspaper with the asterisk next to them at zero down, no security deposit, and no payment for the first month.

- Great credit score: 700 to 759

This range is also attractive to lenders and will still land you a good interest rate.

- Average credit score: 620 to 699

This score will still allow you to obtain credit, especially for a mortgage, and get a decent interest rate. But, you may not receive the zero down or zero percent for the first six months deals based on the creditor.

- Poor credit score: 580 to 619

This rate will allow you to get certain loans, like auto loans, but the lender is absolutely in the driver's seat. In most cases, you will pay twice as much for the item than you should because of your credit score. You will also increase your debt-to-income ratio due to higher-than-expected monthly payment amounts.

- Bad credit score: 580 and below

If your credit score falls somewhere in this range, financing terms will cost you big-time. For long-term loans, such as a thirty-year mortgage, expect to see interest rates that are at least 3 percent higher than interest rates awarded to borrowers with good credit. For shorter-term loans, like a thirty-six-month auto loan, the effects of your bad credit score are even more pronounced. Expect interest rates almost double those offered to consumers with good credit scores.

The big question I receive when talking to individuals about their credit score is what makes up their credit score and how can they increase it. So let's discuss it so you can get to work.

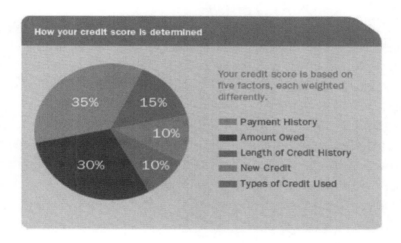

Source: myFICO.com

Graph Description

Payment History (35 percent)

The payment history is the heaviest weighted area when computing your credit score; it's 35 percent of your overall credit score. This area determines how diligent you have been with paying your credit cards, loans, and any others forms of debt. If you pay your debts on a timely basis, this will positively affect your score. The time interval since the last outstanding debt obligation, bankruptcy, and the number of debts all affect your score. You have full control over this area. Start with one card and create good habits. You'll likely get other offers if you pay your bill on time, so be sure you don't get into more debt than you can afford. Credit is not free cash. Just a few missed payments could truly hurt your score. To ensure 100 percent positive pay history make sure you set all credit items up on automatic deduction. To ensure payments always paid even if you get ill or are on travel.

Debt/Amount Owed (30 percent)

This category reflects the amount of money you owe on each of your outstanding debts. It is the proportion of the amount of credit you've been extended (your credit limit) in relation to the amount you've used (your balance) on every account. The total amount of loan installments pending on your accounts is also taken into consideration. Your student or car loans are not evaluated like credit cards. For example if you have a $1,000 credit card and use $700. Then you have utilized 70 percent of your available credit. You want to try not to exceed 30 percent usage, unless your plan is to pay off the entire balance monthly.

Length of History (15 percent)

Establishing good credit from a young age is important. Good credit ensures your name remains in positive standing in relation to your credit history. Interest rates, loan stipulations, and other credit-based terms will be more desirable when you have good credit. A low-risk suggestion for young adults in high school or just entering college is to obtain a credit card with a low limit, around $300-$500. Securing a credit card and paying it back on time every month teaches fiscal responsibility, and also lends understanding to how credit works. Another suggestion, if possible, is to have young adults cosign on an installment loan, such as a car. This too will assist in the process of building solid credit. Credit Karma (www.creditkarma.com) shows you how many years and months you have had credit. A longer credit history can have a more positive impact on your credit because it allows potential creditors to see established patterns and credit usage habits.

Inquiries (10 percent)

After you have applied for your initial few credit cards to establish your credit, you should only apply for credit as needed. Every time you apply for credit it can ding your score a few points. These dings on your credit may remain from six months up to two years. In fact, the more inquires you make, the worse it reflects on your credit. Too many inquiries on your credit report sends signals to lenders that you might not be the most responsible person when it comes to your finances. Multiple inquiries indicate multiple attempts to obtain additional credit sources. If lenders don't believe borrowers are responsible with their finances, they will deny credit requests.

Mix/Types of Credit (10 percent)

A vast mix or different types of credit, comprises about 10 percent of the report. However, it's still viewed by lenders. Again, you don't need a large quantity of credit cards or loans to meet these criteria. If you have a few credit cards, or possibly a small number of installment loans, financial responsibility will be on display for the lender. (Bailey 2013)

Top items that will decrease your score:

1. Late payments

2. Collection accounts and charge offs

3. Filing bankruptcy

- Chapter 7 is normally filed when the person has no way of paying back any of their debt. Anything of value aside from items needed to survive are often sold to help pay off the debts acquired.

- Chapter 13 is available to those who need help reducing their debt to a manageable amount, and plan to make payments over time.

4. Having a home foreclosed

5. Defaulting on students loans

6. Maxed out credit card balances

7. Judgments, liens, and garnishments

8. Closing multiple credit cards all at once

9. Applying for multiple credit cards or loans

10. Not having a balanced list of accounts (credit cards, mortgage, or installment loans)

Reasons to Dispute YOUR Credit Score

Below is a list of reasons people commonly review their credit score:

1. Denied Credit

2. Suspicion of Identity Theft

3. No movement in credit score after paying off debt

How to Dispute a Credit Score

You can get free credit score information from www.myfico.com, www.annualcreditreport.com or www.creditreport.com. If your scores are much lower than expected, carefully review the report. If you find something in your credit history that doesn't make sense, dispute it. This includes credit cards or loans you never applied for or don't currently possess; loan requests made in your name that you were not aware of, or even a misreporting of your income. If any information is incorrect, you have a case to dispute your score. Contact the credit reporting bureaus immediately and explain the mistake, presenting any evidence you may have for your case. With any luck, the credit bureaus will recognize what has happened, remove the offending material from the report, and as a result, your credit score will go up.

You can also file credit report disputes online, go to www.experian.com, www.equifax.com, and www.transunion.com to get more details. If you file them online you can also check the status of your dispute.

Sample Dispute Letter:

Your full name:
Your permanent address:
Present contact number:

Name of credit reporting agency
Address of credit reporting agency

Dear Sir or Madam,

I would like to dispute some inaccurate information I have discovered on my credit report. The items I believe to be incorrect are listed below. I am also including a copy of my credit report with the disputed information highlighted.

Creditor name and account number

Description of the item(s)

Item(s) and an explanation of what you want the credit bureau to do with the information, along with valid proof to support your claim.

In compliance with the Fair Credit Reporting Agency (FCRA), I request that you investigate this matter and update my credit report accordingly.

If your investigation validates the listing, please provide me with an explanation of the procedure you used to validate the listing within fifteen business days of your completion of the investigation, as per the FCRA. I also request that you send me a copy of the information you gathered as a result of the investigation.

If your investigation shows this listing to be erroneous, please update my credit report and send me a copy of my updated credit report.

Sincerely,

Your signature
Your printed name

4

WHO'S IN YOUR LINEUP?

The Power of Five

Without consultation, plans are frustrated, but with many counselors they succeed. (Proverbs 15:22 NASB)

Once you get your budget in place and understand your financial picture, credit report, and score, it's time to build your team. If you want to be successful, then you need to build a team of people who are well-versed in different areas and who you can seek advice from when you have questions or concerns. One individual can only hold but so much knowledge. Also, remember you can only execute to the level of your exposure.

I'm sure you've heard the saying by John C. Maxwell, "Teamwork makes the dream work." Well, if you dream of one day being financially fit, then you need to start identifying your players. Who do you currently do business with? Does your present team primarily consist of close friends and family members? Do they provide facts, half-truths, or opinions? You need people in your circle of success to be knowledgeable, effective communicators, and committed to your financial and personal growth. You may say, "I have my finances under control." But Mattie Stépanek said it best, "Unity is strength...when there is teamwork and collaboration, wonderful things can be achieved." Let people do what they do well and let their expertise work for you.

More important than any question I've asked above, have you consulted with God and bathed your financial aspirations in prayer? Pray that he gives you discernment with your partners as you gain wisdom about your finances. Your current situation is a reflection of you trusting your own decision-making process and your flesh. Keep God at the forefront of your finances moving forward. Philippians 4:19 says, "God will meet all your needs according to His glorious riches in Christ Jesus."

Everyone has needs, goals, and diverse levels of financial knowledge based on our current and past situations and what we've been exposed to. If you ask a group of ten people what it means to be wealthy, I guarantee you'll hear differing definitions. If you asked most teenagers, their responses would likely have something to do with having a big house and owning an expensive car because of what they see on television and in music videos. They don't understand that in most cases, these high-ticket items used in movies and music videos are leased or rented. The actor or artist can't truly afford what they are rapping about.

I asked my wife how she determines wealth. She answered, "Wealth is ensuring that my children are able to attend college debt free, having more money than bills, owning short and long-term investments, building assets through home ownership (including investment properties), the ability to give to those less fortunate, and leaving an inheritance for the next generations." I guess I have rubbed off on her.

Most folks treat their finances as intimate information. Your financial status is most likely not something you disclose freely. In fact, you're probably quite secretive about your monetary status. I see this when I am sitting with couples doing financial counseling. About half of the couples don't understand the financial status of their mate. This is always a sticky place, especially if their finances are out of whack.

As another example, we often don't get the full story when a friend is telling us about their recent too-good-to-be-true acquisition. How many times have you talked with a neighbor, co-worker, or family member about a new car purchase? You're probably remembering the stories now. Your best friend buys a new car and tells you that despite the fact that she has less-than-perfect credit (though she never does say exactly what her score is) she was able to walk onto the lot, pick out the car she wanted, and drive away happy. She makes the deal sound so sweet that you decide it's time for you to buy your dream car too.

Let me caution you here: do not make decisions based on what's worked for others.

Think about the other factors that play a part in car buying. There's the interest rate to consider, the value of the car versus the sticker price, and whether or not there's negative equity (when the value of an asset used to secure a loan is less than the outstanding balance of the loan) to be rolled over into what could be your fresh new ride. Maybe Ms. Brag-A-Lot weighed all these things first; maybe she didn't. The truth is, you don't know, and she's probably not going to tell you because the deal may not have been as sweet as she led you to believe. Instead of unwittingly following in the footsteps of someone who claims to have gotten the loan of a lifetime, always ask yourself the tough questions. In addition, consult those who can help you make informed decisions.

Seek the advice of trained financial professionals when you make major financial decisions. Allow me to introduce you to *The Power of Five,* a concept I came up with to assist you in your personal finances and your business practices. The idea is that there are five people with specialized knowledge or expertise who you consult when you have financial issues or questions. You don't just seek them out when a situation arises, you build relationships with them over time to cultivate trust and loyalty. So who are these five professionals? A tax attorney or Certified Public Accountant (CPA), banker, financial advisor, insurance agent, and an attorney whom you can consult with about general matters. Together, these five individuals create The Power of Five.

Never hire anyone who tells you they can do the job of all five people all by themselves. What's the saying again? "Jack of all trades, master of nothing"? For example, there are many areas of law including employment law, non-profit law, litigation, trademark and patent law, corporate law, bankruptcy law, and so on. There's no way one attorney can specialize in all these areas. So, select one you can confer with about general matters but who can also direct you to another attorney depending on what your needs are.

The Power of Five: Roles + Definitions

1. *Banker*

Role: manage accounts and acquire credit cards and loans

Definition: person employed by a bank, especially as an executive or other official

2. *Lawyer*

Role: write trusts and wills; incorporate businesses

Definition: profession is to give legal advice and assistance to clients and represent them in court or in other legal matters

3. *Financial Advisor*

Role: manage your investments, college savings, mutual funds, stocks and bonds, 401k, etc.

Definition: an individual or an entity who is entrusted with the task of providing advice or counsel to aid the process of investment and asset management

4. Insurance Agent

Role: manage your life, home, personal property, business and vehicle insurance

Definition: an agent of an insurer authorized to negotiate contracts of insurance

5. CPA/Accountant

Role: create your financial statements and prepare your taxes

Definition: an individual who has passed the uniform CPA examination administered by the American Institute Of Certified Public Accountants, and who has received state certification to practice accounting.

The reality is, one day, you will lose a family member. If you have insurance and have built a relationship with your agent, it will be that agent who delivers the check during your time of bereavement with a bucket of southern fried chicken and some side dishes to boot. Or, would you prefer it come in the mail, impersonally, from a company you've been paying for years? If you have questions in the midst of your mourning, would you rather call an 800 number, be likely placed on hold or relegated to pressing numbers on your keypad till you figure out exactly which extension you're supposed to dial, or your insurance agent, your partner, whom you have a personal cell number for? Who better to explain the financial situation and financial matters related to death?

When it's your time to meet the Maker, your attorney should be reading your will, because if he's in your Five, he'll be familiar with you and likely your family too. Knowing the person delivering this kind of news makes an emotional situation much more comfortable. But, you have to build these relationships for them to matter or make a difference.

Here's another situation to think about: How about when you're trying to get a loan and your credit score is a few points lower than required? The banker who knows you will be in a much better position to speak on your behalf than the banker who doesn't. The banker who you have built a relationship with (if he likes you) will recommend your loan for approval. Having these relationships might not sound important to you now, but I assure you, when you're faced with these situations, you'll be glad you have them. Who knows you is important in all the aforementioned scenarios. In the words of Sharon Murphy Williams, Executive Director and Founder of the Phebe Foundation, "It's who knows you, not who you know." Who knows your name?

Again, allow people to do what they do. Do not seek financial advice from individuals who are in the same money situation as you are. Sure, you can swap stories if you wish, but looking to someone to give you advice when he or she is not doing any better than you are is unwise. There is a reason people attend college, take up trades, and pass state test exams. They have areas of specialty. Attorneys must pass the bar exam; CPAs, the CPA exam; financial advisors, the life and health exam, Series 6, 62, 63, 65 and 7. Yes, you can do some research yourself. As a matter-of-fact, you should do some studying on your own. But Googling will only take you so far, as the

Internet will only give you bits and pieces of information, and even then, you have to know what you're looking for.

As you create your own personal Power of Five, it's important that no one person knows your financial status better than you. You have to know your goals better than everyone at the table; your team just helps you get them accomplished. Life happens. Your partners could relocate, retire, or die. Educate yourself. Learn how to ask the right questions. Grow your knowledge base. You should be able to hold a sound financial conversation about your money. No one will be able to take advantage of you if you know your financial standing.

The word relationship is defined as:

- The way in which two or more people, groups, countries, etc., talk to, behave toward, and deal with each other

- The way in which two or more people or things are connected

Know your five individuals by name, not just title. Converse with them frequently enough so that they get to know you and you get to know them. Not only should you have a relationship with your team, but your immediate family should know them as well. Your partners should also be aware of each other, as there will be times when transactions intersect. These five individuals will handle all of your financial affairs. I sometimes discuss my legal matters with my banker and my financial matters with my attorney. Build genuine relationships.

Make sure you interview at least three people with each area of expertise before you settle on the one who will be your partner. Additionally, see the examples below to determine how to choose your Power of Five partners. There are questions listed to assist with choosing your attorney and CPA. These criteria can also be applied when choosing your other partners.

Things to Consider When Choosing Your CPA:

1. **Determine the type of assistance you require** - Stop and think about exactly what you need before you choose an accountant. Some CPAs prefer to stick to more generalized accounting services, such as the preparation of annual financial statements, while others are available for year-round advice and can provide assistance with specified services, including ongoing financial planning and more. If you're a business owner, you may even be able to find an accountant in your area who specializes in your particular industry, such as non-profit or retail accounting. To ensure that you're receiving the best possible help, you will need to choose an accounting firm that focuses on services most beneficial to you. Keep in mind that some financial necessities, such as filing back taxes, may be better suited to a tax attorney. Choose the proper CPA based on your current needs.

2. **Chemistry** - Interview a few CPAs to ensure your level of comfort with the professional you eventually select. After all, you are choosing a person who will handle all of your financial matters. If you have doubts about this person's professionalism, their ability to communicate with you, or your general ability to work together, you could be putting your livelihood at stake. Be sure to ask plenty of questions, so you can get a feel for how the accountant's firm will approach your needs. You need to be at ease with the firm's particular business culture, confident in their ability to give you negative news, assured of their competence when you ask them to accurately assess your financial situation, and their ability to set you up for success.

3. **Competency/Credentials** - It is important to double-check your accountant's accreditation. Where did they receive their education? Are they currently licensed and certified in your state? Also, how many years of experience do they have? If you feel more comfortable entrusting your financial needs to someone with a few years under their belt rather than someone fresh out of school, trust your gut.

4. **References** - Do you know someone who uses an accounting professional? Personal experience is an invaluable resource when it comes to choosing an accounting firm. Don't be afraid to ask others who they've used for their accounting needs and if they'd recommend their services to others. If you desire, you can even ask the firms that you've interviewed to provide you with a list of their most important clients. This will help you get a sense of the quality of the accountant's work.

Questions to ask when choosing your financial advisor:

1. **What is your educational background and what experience do you have?** Find out what areas of study your advisor has pursued, how long they've been in practice, and how many and what types of companies the advisor has been associated with. Ask the advisor to describe her work experience and how it relates to her current practice.

2. **What are your qualifications and what do you do to stay current in the field?** Ask the advisor what qualifies him or her to offer financial advice. Determine whether he or she is recognized as a **Certified Financial Planner™ (CFP®).** If she says she is, verify her current certification, in addition to whether she has ever been disciplined by the Certified Financial Planner™ Board of Standards. Find out if the advisor ever

personally filed for bankruptcy protection. You can locate this information by visiting www.cfp.net.

3. **What services do you offer?** The services a financial advisor offers depends on a number of factors including credentials, licenses, and areas of expertise. Financial advisors cannot sell insurance or securities products like mutual funds or stocks, without proper licenses. Nor can they give investment advice unless they are registered with their state or with the Securities and Exchange Commission. You can locate this information at www.sec.gov. Through this website, you are able to determine if your advisor and their firm are licensed, plus whether they have any disciplinary complaints or actions against them. To find out if someone is licensed to sell insurance, Google your state's department of insurance, and look for the consumer page.

4. **How can I pay for your services and how much do you typically charge?** Per your agreement, the advisor should clearly tell you in writing how she will be paid for the services provided. Fees are charged either by the hour, as a flat rate, or as a percentage of your assets and/or net worth and commissions. While the amount you pay the advisor may depend on your particular needs, the advisor should be able to provide you with an estimate of possible costs based on the work to be performed.

5. **Can I have it in writing?** Ask the advisor to provide you with a written agreement that details the services that will be provided. Make sure you read it carefully then reread it. Don't just toss it in the recycle bin. You'll want to pay attention to all the fine print and ask for clarification on anything you don't thoroughly understand. Keep this document in your files for future reference.

Here are some additional questions you should consider when selecting your partners:

1. What is their specialty?

2. How closely will I need to be involved in my partner's work?

3. Can I hire a partner to handle only certain parts of my financial matters?

4. What is in the fee agreement?

5. How does a partner decide what to charge?

6. What additional out-of-pocket costs will I have to pay?

7. When is my partner's bill due?

Here are additional resources to assist you in locating partners:

www.lawyers.com

www.cpadirectory.com

www.insuranceagents.com

When choosing your partners make sure you utilize the list of C's previously mentioned. My CEO, Dr. Vernon, makes use of and has trained our hiring staff to use these same qualifications when hiring staff members. This concept originated with Bill Hybel, author of "Courageous Leadership." The three C's—character, chemistry, and competence—are critical and should never be comprised. Sacrificing any of the three C's may lead to regrets.

Also, when choosing a partner don't always let price be the driving factor. Like the saying goes, you get what you pay for. And remember, most things are negotiable, so if the fee of a person you're interested in working with is a little higher than what you can afford to pay, try to talk them down in a way that shows you respect their level of expertise and the right they've earned to charge more because of it.

Okay, now that you have the information you need to know on what questions to ask, get started! Go to a networking event, acquire business cards, shake hands, introduce yourself, make calls, and set appointments. It's time for your financial relationships and your money to go to the next plane. If you wouldn't refer a potential partner to your closest family member, then keep searching.

In the following chapters, I will attempt to ensure when you choose your Power of Five you will be equipped to have conversations, know what questions to ask and understand some of the products that will assist you with your financial affairs in their various areas. The following chapters will discuss types of insurances, important legal documents, financial institutions and the products offered; as well as, tax information and investment products. Go out and build relationships. Locate your attorney, banker, tax accountant or CPA, insurance agent and financial advisor. I know you can sometimes be around people who will give you advice or have good ideas. Nevertheless, please don't confuse good ideas and advice as an exchange for expertise. May God be with you on this journey!

5

RAISE YOUR HAND IF YOU'RE INSURED

Insurance Explained

Good planning and hard work lead to prosperity, but hasty shortcuts lead to poverty. (Proverbs 21:5 NLT)

If you're a parent, husband, wife, or custodian of another loved one, then I probably don't have to explain to you the importance of protecting your family. You'd sooner sacrifice a limb than knowingly compromise their safety. What you may not understand, however, is that if you don't have health insurance, short-term and long-term disability insurance, and life insurance, long-term care, mortgage, renters, and auto insurance you are putting the very ones you care about at risk. Of course, you wouldn't intentionally jeopardize the welfare, financial wellbeing, or future of anyone who is important to you. But if you lack any one of the coverages I just mentioned, then I must apologize for being the one to have to break the news to you: that's exactly what you're doing. You're gambling and putting yourself in financial jeopardy, which means your family is at risk by association.

Unless you are filthy rich and have no problem paying all your medical and related expenses out of pocket, you need insurance. These are areas most people don't discover the importance of until they are truly needed. If you're like "most people," then I have more bad news for you: if you don't pay now, you will pay later. Not investing in protecting your life or the lives of your loved ones will adversely affect one or all of you at some point in time. I'm not trying to scare you (*or maybe I am*), but I do want you to realize the gravity of the consequences of not having insurance.

A large portion of medical expenses can be offset with the preventive measure of maintaining good health, so here's a tip: take care of yourself by eating and exercising on a regular basis.

I must inform you that one of the most common collection accounts on the average credit report is medical expenses. According to the

Federal Reserve, over 50 percent of collection records and 20 percent of lawsuits that appear on credit reports are related to medical debts. Medical bills often rack up when a person has no health insurance. In an article titled "Medical Bill Nightmares" by Emily Davidson she stated the following:

Medical debts impact not only the uninsured but the insured as well.

• Uninsured patients – Over 45 million Americans (15 percent of the population) don't have medical insurance. Nearly half of people without medical insurance currently have outstanding medical debts, averaging $9,000 per person.

• Insured patients – Over 60 percent of families who report having medical debt problems are covered by medical insurance. In fact, 75 percent of people who filed for bankruptcy because of medical debts had health insurance.

The truth is, unless you're in the top percentage of earners in this country and you're already debt free, those expenses will amount to much more than what you can afford, all things considered. For example, on average, the birth of a child in America costs $30,000 for a vaginal delivery and $50,000 for a C-section, with commercial insurers paying out an average of $18,329 and $27,866, according to an article written by Elizabeth Rosenthal in June 2013, published in the Health section of the New York Times. How many people do you know with $30,000-$50,000 sitting around?

Currently, our nation is bearing witness to a major shift in political and social policy as it relates to healthcare reform. The Patient Protection and Affordable Care Act was signed into law on March 23, 2010. Open enrollment began on October 1, 2013. This legislation, largely regarded as President Obama's most significant win while in office, revolutionized the way we in America think about and receive medical coverage.

Familiarize yourself with Affordable Care Act because whether you need to visit the Health Insurance Marketplace to shop for coverage or not, as a US citizen, the ACA (Affordable Care Act) does affect you. The (simple) goal of the program is to make sure everyone in America has access to affordable healthcare. "We took up the fight because we believe that, in America, nobody should have to worry about going broke just because somebody in their family or they got sick...We believe that nobody should have to choose between putting food on their kids' table or taking them to see the doctor," President Obama said in a speech given at The White House on December 3, 2013.

As of March 2014, almost every person must have health insurance coverage of some sort, or face steadily rising penalties. Businesses with fifty or more employees who work at least thirty hours a week must provide affordable healthcare or be penalized. Small business owners also have to provide healthcare, but the stipulations are different and provisions are made in the form of federal tax credits to counter costs. There's a lot to learn about this new legislation—far too much to cover in this book—but trust me, you'll want to do your research to know what the implications are for you.

When key parts of this new health care law take effect in 2014, there will be a new way to buy health insurance: the Health Insurance Marketplace.

The Health Insurance Marketplace is designed to help you find health insurance that meets your needs and fits your budget. The Marketplace offers "one-stop shopping" to find and compare private health insurance options. You may also be eligible for a tax credit that lowers your monthly premium right away.

You may qualify to save money and lower your monthly premium, but only if your employer does not offer coverage, or offers coverage that doesn't meet certain standards. The savings on your premium that you're eligible for depends on your household income.

If you have an offer of health coverage from your employer that meets certain standards, you will not be eligible for a tax credit through the Marketplace and may wish to enroll in your employer's health plan. However, you may be eligible for a tax credit that lowers your monthly premium or a reduction in certain cost-sharing if your employer does not offer coverage to you at all or does not offer coverage that meets certain standards. If the cost of a plan from your employer that would cover you (and not any other members of your family) is more than 9.5 percent of your household income for the year, or if the coverage your employer provides does not meet the "minimum value" standard set by the ACA, you may be eligible for a tax credit.

If you purchase a health plan through the Marketplace instead of accepting health coverage offered by your employer, then you may lose the employer contribution (if any) to the employer-offered coverage. Another important distinction to be aware of is that this employer contribution—as well as your employee contribution to employer-offered coverage—is often excluded from income for Federal and State income tax purposes. Your payments for coverage through the Marketplace are made on an *after-tax* basis. For more information about the ACA visit www.healthcare.gov or http://www.whitehouse.gov/healthreform.

The next type of insurance we're going to discuss is life insurance. Life insurance is a way to protect your family in the event of your death. It can also be used as a vehicle to build wealth. Numerous cultures and families make use of life insurance to transfer wealth throughout generations. The money your beneficiaries receive, tax-free, can be used to help pay your final expenses, take care of debt, and cover or eliminate a mortgage and pay for a family member's college education.

Pertaining to life insurance, as the CFO and Chief of Staff of a mega ministry with over 35,000 members, I have witnessed countless cases in which a family loses someone, only to find out that their loved one didn't prepare for his or her death. Worrying about money only compounds grief. You shouldn't have to worry about selling family valuables to pay for funeral costs. Family members shouldn't have to pass the collection plate to raise funds to bury you. The death of a man shouldn't mean more debt for his wife.

In the end, funeral expenses sometimes turn into the obligation of one or two family members who are doing well financially. This is a burden to those individuals, and too often a common occurrence. No one is able to properly mourn when they are pressured by mounting funeral and burial expenses, joint credit card bills left behind, and other debts, with those companies and creditors to whom money is owed demanding to be paid. These distractions only exacerbate and cause what is already an emotionally taxing situation to become a financially taxing one too.

But, it doesn't have to be. The very purpose of life insurance is to take care of these responsibilities and assure your family's needs are provided for. Don't allow the lack of life insurance to tear your family apart. Don't cause your spouse or your children to have to change their entire lifestyle because of your lack of preparation. Without the deceased spouse's income and no insurance proceeds, you'll likely have to downsize, possibly losing the home you were accustomed to living in, the car you were used to driving, and other luxuries (or necessities) you enjoyed when your spouse was alive. They're already grieving because they've lost you; you don't want your family to be doubly devastated because they're also losing things that make them comfortable, especially at a time like the one we're describing. Dr. Vernon often jokes that when he dies, his family won't know whether to cry or shout for joy. That is because he has prepared for the event of his death. His family is protected. Regardless of whether you're a single mother with only one child or a father with a wife and five kids, you should leave your family financially secure. The Bible instructs us on what to do in this matter. Proverbs 13:22 (NASB) says, "A good man leaves an inheritance to his children's children, and the wealth of the sinner is stored up for the righteous."

There are several reasons why people don't purchase insurance. One of the main reasons is because they don't understand it and we often fear what we don't understand. Another reason is people are unaware of the various products available. Also, insurance agents in general, have garnered a bad rep. Some people have had bad experiences with agents and now believe most of them are shady, selling unneeded products to people who can't afford them, in order to collect a commission. Another reason people don't buy life insurance? Because the idea of committing to something that is not readily tangible is not all that enticing. Also, many people think life insurance is something that only old folk purchase. And the biggest reason is that most people have not been educated on this matter by their parents or family members.

You won't be the sucker to be swindled by some scheming scam artist. When you set up your family's future, you'll be informed. You'll know just what questions to ask and what answers to listen for. You'll have enough information to know just about what you want when you walk through the door. All you'll really need is information on which options are available to you from this particular, well-reputed agent. Take notes beforehand so you are prepared for the appointment. Make some bullet points; have your questions ready.

What you need to know about life insurance policies

Purchase a policy with a premium you can afford. It's better to start with a lower benefit amount, then increase it as your income and expenses allow. Otherwise, if you purchase more than you can manage to pay, your policy will lapse and you're going to be without life insurance all over again. Now, what sense would it make to go through all that hassle, researching and comparing companies, and getting poked with needles (oh yes, there will be blood) just to lose it? Not to mention, if anything happens with your health since the time you secured your initial policy, you may not be eligible for the same rate you would have been eligible for (had you only aimed for something reasonable) when you try to have it reinstated. Save yourself unnecessary headache by starting off with a low premium. You can always increase it later. When it comes to purchasing an insurance policy I recommend that you work with your insurance agent to figure out what your needs are and what you can afford; each individual has a different situation.

TYPES OF LIFE INSURANCE

Term Life Insurance

Term life insurance provides protection for a specific period of time, hence the name *term*. It is most often sold in ten, fifteen, twenty, and thirty year terms. The premium stays the same throughout the term. If the insured person dies during this period, the beneficiaries receive the proceeds income-tax free. At the end of each term, the insured may renew the policy (generally at a higher cost) up to age ninety-five.

Advantages and Disadvantages of Term life insurance

Advantages:

Term life insurance can provide essential protection for your family.

- It is **less expensive** than other life insurance options.

- The saying goes, "Buy term and invest the rest." Don't buy a whole life policy unless you can afford the expense; buy term insurance. It's cheaper and you can take the additional money and invest it in a product like a Roth IRA. Consult your financial advisor for further advice.

- You can convert many term life insurance policies into a permanent insurance product such as whole life insurance, universal life insurance or variable universal life insurance.

Disadvantages:

- The downside of term life insurance is that it isn't a permanent life insurance solution.

- Once the term ends, the coverage ends or the premiums increase dramatically.

- As your age increases, the more expensive term gets. In many cases, the individual can't afford to continue the policy, so it lapses. For example, at age twenty-five you buy a twenty year term. You live to forty-five and the term expires. You can increase the term at that point, but now that you are twenty years older, your premiums are higher in cost, and hopefully, you don't have any medical issues preventing you from being insured.

- If you die during the term your coverage is solid and your family is insured. Otherwise, at renewal, the continuing coverage could be out of your price range.

- If you want to purchase another policy after your term ends, you may have to show evidence of good health to purchase continued protection.

Keep in mind that as your life changes (marriage, childbirth, promotions, etc.) so will your life insurance needs. You should weigh any associated costs before making a purchase. There are life insurance fees related to gender, health, and age. There are additional charges for "riders" that customize policies to fit your individual needs.

Whole Life Insurance- Fixed Rate of Interest

Whole life is the most common type of permanent life insurance and is designed for the long term. Before purchasing, be sure to think about your ability to make premium payments (which will remain the same) consistently over the life of the policy. You can choose how often you'd like to make premium payments too, annually, semiannually, quarterly, or monthly. You should base the frequency of your payments on your budget. This will ensure payment of premiums in a timely manner.

Some whole life policies can be paid in full after a certain number of years. When you purchase a policy, you should be informed of the rate of growth related to cash value over the life of your policy. According to Wikipedia, the cash value of an insurance contract, also called cash surrender value, is the cash amount offered to the policy owner by the issuing life carrier upon cancellation of the contract.

Advantages and Disadvantages of Whole Life Insurance

Advantages:

- Easy to understand

- Payments are the same every month

- Some whole life policies can be completely paid for after a certain number of years

- The fixed rate of interest makes it easy to predict the growth of your cash value over time

- Predictable and dependable

Disadvantages:

- Whole life insurance isn't flexible

- You can't customize it

Universal Life Insurance

Universal life insurance provides permanent life insurance protection and access to cash values that grow tax-deferred. The major advantage of universal life insurance is flexibility. You can change the protection level of the policy (within bounds), and you control the amount and frequency of payments (again, within bounds).

Universal life insurance offers protection for your family and strategies for leaving a financial legacy. It can also assist small business owners with continuation planning. It's always best for the business to continue its operations beyond the owner's existence. So, this is important if you have built a business that you would like to be passed down for generations within your family.

Advantages and Disadvantages of Universal Life Insurance

Advantages:

- A universal life insurance policy has the flexibility to adjust to your changing needs

- Your policy's cash value earns interest based on a contractually-stated financial index (or a blend of indices). See glossary for further clarity of what a financial index is. This growth is tax-deferred.

- You can access your cash value at almost any time.

A few important factors to consider when purchasing a UL policy:

- Not FDIC or NCUSIF insured so you would not be entitled to the insurance that is described in the definitions below.

    o FDIC (Federal Deposit Insurance Corporation) - Investopedia defines FDIC as a U.S. corporation that insures deposits in the US against bank failure. Put in place to maintain public confidence and encourage stability in the financial system through the promotion of sound banking practices. Typically insures up to

$250,000 per customer per institution, as long as the bank is a member institution.

o NCUSIF (National Credit Union Share Insurance Fund) - Investopedia defines NCUSIF as a fund monitored by the NCUA (National Credit Union Association) to protect and insure the deposits of federally insured credit union members. Similar to the FDIC, it only insures up to $250,000 per member per institution.

o Visit www.fdic.gov and www.ncua.gov for more info.

• Not guaranteed by the financial institution purchased

• Not insured by any federal government agency

• May lose value due to market fluctuations

• Loans and partial surrenders from a MEC (Modified Endowment Contract) will generally be taxable. If taken prior to age 59 ½ they may be subject to a 10 percent tax penalty.

• Loans and partial surrenders will reduce cash value and any death benefits payable.

Variable Insurance - Includes Investments

Variable universal life insurance is a life insurance product with investment features. It's designed to help you protect your family's future with life insurance. It provides access to professionally managed investments that help you accumulate money for your future needs.

You can use the policy for many of your planned financial needs, such as: supplemental retirement planning solutions, business planning solutions, long-term care, and education funding.

Advantages and Disadvantages of Variable Life Insurance

Advantages:

- You can take advantage of potential market growth because your policy value is invested in underlying sub-accounts which are subject to market fluctuations

- Your policy also has the flexibility to adjust to your changing needs

Disadvantages:

- A variable universal life policy puts greater responsibility on the purchaser. You assume the investment risk and you select and monitor your own underlying investment options instead of the insurance company doing it for you.

Make sure that as your life evolves, these strategies and products are suitable for your long-term life insurance needs. Ensure that you are able to continue premium payments to prevent your policy from lapsing if the market goes down.

Methods of Accessing Cash:

- **Loan** - the ability to borrow money from the issuer using money from the cash accumulation account as collateral. Depending on the terms of the policy you may be assessed interest at a varying rate. You don't have to qualify for a loan, it is approved based on the cash available within the cash accumulation account and is based on the policy terms.

- **Withdrawal** - The amount available differs based on the type of policy and the company issuing it. In most cases, withdrawals are non-taxable up to the policy basis, as long as the contract is not classified as a MEC. Can reduce your death benefit, and can be taxable in some cases if done within the first fifteen years of the contract, of if the withdrawals exceed the policy basis.

- **Partial surrender** - Take cash from the policy, reduce the right to the death benefit protection afforded by the insurance. It reduces the death benefit by the amount that is withdrawn. At some point will have to increase premium because the death benefit was based on a certain cash value being there earning interest. Remember this option is utilized for investment purposes; see your new financial advisor for further information.

- **Whole surrender** – This option will cancel the policy. If you surrender in the early years, you will probably receive surrender fees, reducing your cash value. Varies based on length of ownership. The gain from the policy will be taxable. If you have any loans against the policy additional taxes may prevail.

Investing involves market risk, including the possible loss of principal. Also, know that underlying investment options are only available in variable annuity and variable life insurance contracts. They are not offered directly to the public. Protections and guarantees are subject to the claims-paying ability of the issuing life insurance company. Taking money from your policy immediately reduces both the cash value and the death benefit payable, and can cause the need for more premiums to be paid into the policy in the future. You should always take care to ensure that your life insurance needs continue to be met over time subsequent to taking cash from your policy.

Variable products are sold by prospectus, also known as an offer document. Investopedia defines a prospectus as a formal legal document, which is required by and filed with the Securities and Exchange Commission that provides details about an investment offering for sale to the public. This document provides information and facts that an investor needs to make an informed investment decision.

Before you invest, you should read the prospectus carefully and consider investment objectives, risks, charges, and expenses. The product prospectus and underlying fund prospectus contain this and other important information. Investing involves risk. Investment products are not FDIC-insured, may lose value, and have no bank guarantee.

HEALTH INSURANCE

As previously mentioned, medical expenses, along with student loans, are some of the most common unpaid debts on most credit reports. If your employer offers health coverage, take it! It's like not participating in the 401k, especially when your employer does a match. It's like leaving free money on the table. If your employer offers various plans, evaluate them and purchase the one that best fits your current health status. If you rarely go to the doctor's office because you are in great shape and take great care of yourself, then you may be able to save some money and get a higher-deductible plan. But just because you are in great shape doesn't mean you don't have to get an annual checkup at the least. If you are married, decide what plan best suits your family based on offerings and price.

As the employee you are responsible for a portion of the cost, but the care that you and your family will receive when ill, is worth it. Health insurance includes health, dental, and vision insurance. Dental insurance covers all dental procedures, and vision covers all optical procedures and eyeglasses or contact lenses. If healthcare is not offered by your employer or you are self-employed, visit www.healthcare.gov.

Consumers contact:

Call: 1-800-318-2596

TTY: 1-855-889-4325

Small Business Resources:

Call: 1-800-706-7893

TTY: 1-800-706-7915

Illnesses rarely announce themselves, so it is always important to be prepared; obtain health insurance. Healthcare costs are extremely expensive. With coverage, you have secure health assistance whenever you need it. Healthcare coverage helps to prevent most exorbitant expenses that may occur in the future.

Things to Know About Health Insurance

Health insurances depend on the agreements made between the insurer and benefactor. Some insurers cover a wide range of things, including hospitalization bills of family members, while others do not. There are also insurers that cover large amounts in assisting a person with financial hardships. It is crucial that you review your policy specifics, so you clearly understand what is paid by the insurance company, versus what your obligation is. Being knowledgeable about your financial responsibility when it comes to your medical expenses will enable you to know how much you need to save for a rainy day. The health insurance premium is a payment that should be deducted by payroll and automatic deduction.

Benefits of Health Insurance

Health insurance reduces big expenses you might encounter in the future. Hospital bills can be surprisingly (or not so surprisingly) high. Health insurance is your preparation for the unexpected. Healthcare coverage will also save you out-of-pocket expenses on medications. For doctor visits and prescriptions, most of the time you will only need to pay your deductible or a copay representing a fraction of the actual cost; Moreover, having an insurance plan serves as financial and health security for family members.

Don't get me wrong—I'm all for experimenting with safe, holistic alternatives when you get sick. It's common knowledge that most men don't like to go to the doctor anyway. But the truth is, doctors are trained professionals whom God has blessed with the talent and skill to diagnose and treat all kinds of illnesses, and sometimes, seeing a doctor at a particular point in time can be the difference between life and death. We all know someone or have heard it said about someone, "If they had only caught it early..." Health insurance allows you to go to the doctor when you need to, preventing you from avoiding the hospital because you can't pay for it.

Do your research and choose a policy that covers your immediate family, that is, your spouse and children. Cousin Bonita and Uncle Larry will need to find their own insurance, but you now have enough info to help them make informed decisions about their coverage.

Also, health insurances can also assist with laboratory fees, diagnostic services, mental health care, urgent, and emergency care. These are some of the benefits available to you with healthcare coverage. Furthermore, dental, vision, and other health-related services are accessible through many healthcare insurers. It would be nice if there was one plan that covered everything, but the reality is, medical, vision, and dental insurance are typically discrete, so you'll have to research all three to find the coverage that's right for you.

Importance of Health Care

Healthcare is a good investment. It allows you to have options and choose your physician. It lowers your immediate financial commitment due to expensive healthcare costs. Like other forms of insurance, it is a safety net. It will save you plenty of money. For example, if you have a baby on the way, health insurance can definitely help to offset some of the expenses, as medical costs continue to rise. Having insurance lessens your chances of being placed in collections. With this being said, according to www.ebri.org, fifty million nonelderly Americans (or 18.9 percent) were uninsured.

SHORT-TERM AND LONG-TERM DISABILITY INSURANCE

While many protect their families by purchasing life insurance, disability insurance is a type of protection that is often bypassed. Disability insurance allows you to provide a regular income for you and your family if you are unable to work because you're incapacitated. Disability insurance can be either short or long term. In some cases, your employer may offer both of these options as a part of your overall plan.

Short-Term Disability Insurance

Short-term disability insurance is a type of coverage that kicks in almost immediately after you've become disabled. If provided through your employer, contact your benefits administrator to determine the waiting period, which is typically up to fourteen days. Benefits are paid from several months up to one year, but sometimes even up to two years depending on policy stipulations. You are covered for the time designated by your particular policy, not to exceed a predetermined maximum benefit amount provided with your policy, or until you recover.

With short-term disability insurance, you can receive a benefit that is equal to a specific percentage of your salary. For instance, you might receive a benefit that is equal to 60 percent of your pre-disability salary. So, if you earned $500 per week working, you will then receive $300 per week per your disability coverage. The money you receive can be used to pay bills until long-term disability kicks in, or until you get back to work.

The downside of short-term disability coverage is that illnesses and disabilities are harder to prove. You'll likely have to go through extensive application processes, fill out tons of paperwork, and on top of that, depending on your particular disability, get verification from several doctors or medical professionals. Another thing that sucks about short-term disability is that you may not receive benefits when you actually need them. But better late than never, right? You still need it nonetheless.

Examples of reasons for Short Term Disability payout:

• A lengthy illness

• Disabling injury

• Birth of a child

Long-Term Disability Insurance

Long-term disability insurance is similar to short-term, except for the timeframe in which it is used. They both assist with replacing a portion of your income lost due to the inability to perform your current job duties. A long-term disability insurance policy may take effect between three months and one year after you've become disabled. Once you start to receive benefits from this kind of policy, you can receive benefits for a specific number of years, or until you reach the age of sixty-five. Like short-term disability insurance, you'll also receive a percentage of your pre-disability income. These benefits can be paid in full even if you have to take a job that pays significantly less than what you made before the disability. If your new income is less than 20 percent of what you made prior, you can usually receive benefits from the policy. When you get an individual long-term policy, it is typically a guaranteed, renewable policy, which allows you to renew as long as you pay the premiums.

When dealing with insurances, don't cut corners. These types of policies will protect you and your family in cases of death or sudden disability. Not having health insurance can leave you with a pile of expensive medical bills. Lack of life insurance could cause your spouse or family to have to immediately sell assets to survive, or they may need to drastically change their lifestyle. Short and long-term disability insurance will provide you with a portion of your income while you're out of work recovering from a disability. I recommend that you purchase both short and long-term insurance, due to the waiting period for long-term disability insurance being at least ninety days. The average person has less than one month's expenses in their account, so without short-term disability insurance this could cause you a tremendous financial hardship.

Start with your employer when considering the purchase of these products, but I advise you to purchase life insurance individually as well. If you are able to purchase life insurance through your employer, in most cases the policy will not be transferrable, which means that if you leave that employer, your policy will be void.

Also, the older you get, the higher the premiums get. So, if you purchase an insurance policy from your employer and you are employed there for thirty-five years and you decide to retire or leave the company that policy ceases. If you were thirty years old when you started but now you are sixty-five, that same policy will be much more expensive. Hopefully, you haven't acquired any illness such as diabetes, lupus, or cancer, or it could be almost impossible to get any insurance.

Examples of Long-Term Disability Insurance payout:

1. Cancer

2. Mental Disorder

3. Heart Attack

4. Injuries

5. Osteoarthritis

Long-Term Care Insurance

Long-term care insurance pays for a portion or all costs of caregiving needed due to physical or cognitive disability. Like other policies, pricing will be based on health and age and other factors based on the carrier. This policy will cover and reimburse costs for care received at home or at an assisted living or skilled nursing facility. The waiting period for this type of policy is thirty to one hundred-eighty days; usually, the longer the waiting period, the lower the premium.

In an article written for CNN Money by Blake Ellis, he says that in the past five years, the median annual cost of private nursing home care has jumped 24 percent from $67,527 to $83,950, according to Genworth's 2013 Cost of Care Survey, based on data from nearly fifteen thousand long-term care providers. From 2012 to 2013 alone, the price climbed 4 percent. If you don't have a long-term care insurance policy in place, the cost of your care could possibly wipe all your assets away due to the high costs.

Mortgage Insurance

Mortgage insurance is a financial guaranty for the lender that will help to reduce or eliminate a loss in the case of a default by the borrower, defined by www.bankrate.com. Sometimes referred to as PMI (Private Mortgage Insurance), unless you are paying for your house cash, most banks now require that you escrow your mortgage insurance, especially if you put down less than a 20 percent down payment on your home or you are refinancing to more than 80 percent of your home's value.

Bankrate.com goes on to say that PMI is based on your down payment and the mortgage loan amount, and can vary between .39 of a percent to 1.15 percent of the loan. If you have an FHA (Federal Housing Authority) guaranteed loan, you could be responsible for mortgage insurance for up to five years, unless you refinance to a conventional loan after a year of having the loan. If you acquire a conventional loan unless you have 20-22 percent of equity in your home you will be responsible for PMI payments.

PMI Calculations

Loan Amount – Loan Balance = Equity

If you purchase a home for $100,000 and make a 22 percent down payment, you will only need to borrow $78,000. In most cases you will not be responsible for PMI payments because you will immediately have 22 percent equity in your home.

If you purchase a home for $100,000 and make a 10 percent down payment, you borrow $90,000. The mortgage insurer charges an annual premium of 0.53 percent. The insurer multiplies the loan amount by 0.0053, for an annual premium of $477.00, which is divided into twelve monthly payments of $39.75.

If you move in and do large renovations, I would recommend that you request to have a new appraisal conducted (at your cost) to have the PMI removed. If the appraisal states you have less than 80 percent loan-to-value ratio, or 20-22 percent in equity it will reduce your monthly house payment once PMI is removed. If it is removed, use this savings to go toward your principal only payment to continue to reduce your mortgage debt. PMI insurance allows the bank and the insurance company to share in the risk of the home. Also, home owners can write off the cost of mortgage insurance on their taxes.

Renters Insurance

When my wife and I were renters, we had renters insurance from our first year of college till we bought our first home. It cost us less than twenty dollars a month. I had the insurance company do an automatic deduction of my monthly payment to ensure I made this payment on time. By doing the automatic deduction it also saved us two dollars a month on our payment.

Investopedia defines renters insurance as a form of property insurance that provides coverage for a policy owner belongings and liability within a rental property. Renters insurance applies to persons renting or leasing a single family home, apartment, duplex, condo, studio, loft, or townhome.

Most people think that when they rent or lease, the property owner's insurance will cover the cost if something happens to their personal belongings. That is not the case. It would cover the property itself and if the renter is uninsured it would be an out-of-pocket loss. Insure your valuables and the security of your family.

For example, if a fire were to occur, you'd want your insurance to put you in a hotel and pay all your expenses while you wait to return home. This will prevent you from having to contact a family member and put them in a tough position. In some cases, based on the extent of the damage you won't know the length of time it will take to make repairs.

On www.usnews.com, it was stated that according to a recent Rent.com survey, 60 percent of renters do not have a renters insurance policy. Younger renters were even less likely to be covered, with 72 percent under the age of twenty-five without a policy. Even though the sixty-five and older set were most likely to have insurance (51 percent), that number isn't as high as you'd expect for a population that's accumulated a lifetime of assets (Article: Why You Can't Afford to Skip Renters Insurance by Niccole Schreck).

The small cost of renters insurance will not equate to the high cost of replacing all your personal belongings in the event of a flood, fire, or theft. Most people just think that it's not necessary and/or they can't afford it, most people don't realize how many things they accumulate over the years until they lose it in a fire and have to replace them.

Homeowners Insurance

Wikipedia defines homeowners insurance, also known as a hazard or multiple line insurance, as a type of insurance that protects a private residence. It combines various personal insurance protections, which can include losses occurring to one's home, its contents, loss of use, or loss of other personal possessions that belong to the homeowner, as well as liability insurance for accidents that may happen at the home or at the hands of the homeowner within the policy territory.

The cost of the homeowners insurance is based on the cost to replace the home, endorsements, or riders that are a part of the policy. Ensure that you verify the limits and availability of features such as fire, flood, and theft protection, and what type of coverage is available even in the event of your death. Some of these items, if not included in the actual policy, have to be added to the policy as a rider. We have all heard many tragic stories on the local news where homeowners have experienced an unexpected house fire, flood, or burglary and they lose everything in a matter of minutes or just a few hours.

As an example, you want to ensure you have a flood or drain backup rider on your policy, especially if you live in a flood zone. Discuss available riders with your insurance agent, and additional endorsements to ensure to cover all your assets under all allowable circumstances. When people are unprepared, the Salvation Army or Red Cross and other local community-based organizations are forced to step in and give them temporary housing, food, and clothing. But, the assistance offered by these organizations is only a Band-Aid, which is why this type of insurance is a must.

Remember, in the average American's case their home will be their biggest investment and largest asset. You would hate to lose what you worked your entire career to pay off due to lack of insurance. This insurance is a must as long as you are a homeowner, even after the home is paid in full.

Auto Insurance

In most states, auto insurance is mandatory. Show financial responsibility as a driver and purchase at least the state minimum limits, which you can gather from your insurance agent or by visiting your state's department of insurance website. You can visit the Ohio insurance site at www.insurance.ohio.gov. On this site you can find the following data: required minimum for Bodily Injury Liability Coverage was $12,500 per person injured in any one accident and $25,000 for all persons injured in any one accident. The required minimum for Property Damage Liability Coverage was $7,500 for injury to or destruction of property of others in any one accident. In December 2013, new law raised the minimum limits to $25,000 per person injured in any one accident with a $50,000 maximum for all persons injured in any one accident. The minimum Property Damage Coverage will be $25,000 for property of others.

As of December 2013, in Ohio, the law now requires companies to begin issuing policies with these new limits for new and renewal business. Consider that as of August 2013, according to an article by Janet Loehrke and Anne Carey, the average cost of a car was $31,252, up from $30,300 in 2012.

So, imagine if you had a policy with the old property limit of $7,500 and you hit a 2014 Nissan Sentra, and that the average cost of that Nissan according to www.nissan.com was $17,500. In this case, your insurance wouldn't cover the cost. The victim or their insurance would then in most cases sue you in court for the difference of around $10,000, which you would be personally responsible for.

Protect your assets and purchase a policy with limits that will cover your assets. With high deductibles, you want to ensure that you have the necessary cash to cover it in your rainy day fund. We can all attest to a friend who got in an accident and is still driving around with the dent or damage. The damage was less than the deductible and the individual couldn't afford the repair.

Remember, low deductibles and appropriate coverage limits are what's most important, not the state limits. Especially until you have enough at all times to cover the deductible amount.

Your auto-insurance payment is another bill that should be put on automatic deduction, first, so that the policy doesn't lapse because you forgot to put the check in the mail and second, you may receive a discount on your policy for paying this way. You don't want to get caught without car insurance, but not having this coverage can cause you to lose everything due to a lawsuit, and then on top of that, there is the added possibility of receiving a ticket and being summoned to appear in court to present proof of insurance.

When purchasing your auto, home, and renters insurance policies make sure you don't just get the lowest limits. You want to ensure that you cover your assets. Remember, the amount that you don't cover with insurance you could possibly be sued for in civil court.

Sometimes, we go for the cheapest premium which in most cases, especially when you're younger, are lower coverages and high deductibles. All of these policies can be discussed with your insurance broker. Multiple policies with the same provider will land you a discount in most cases.

6

PAY YOUR PART

Personal Tax Information

Render to all what is due them: tax to whom tax is due; custom to whom custom; fear to whom fear; honor to whom honor. (Romans 13:7 NASB)

When it comes to managing your finances, I can't think of many items more important than filing your taxes every year. If you're a business owner, you should be filing every quarter. The Internal Revenue Service (IRS) is one organization that should be high on your list of priorities, actually at the top. Pay your taxes on time and in truth. Filing taxes is a responsibility almost every working person has, and not taking care of this responsibility in particular can cost you big time.

When tax season rolls around, most people just take their W-2s to a local tax company or national chain like H&R Block to file and haven't a clue what their taxes consist of. Understanding what financial activities and documents should be taken into consideration from the previous year could make a huge difference in your bottom line.

Let's break down what your 2014 filing status and tax bracket is. You can always go to irs.gov to see the updated tax bracket charts for the current year.

What do you know about your taxes besides what's reflected on your W-2 or 1099? Is the size of your federal tax refund the only thing you care about? I've got news for you. There are actually some other —dare I say it?—more important things to consider. Let's talk about them and get a clear understanding about what filing taxes is really all about. And from this point on, I want you to stop getting your taxes filed only to sign the documents, send them off, and toss copies in some file without reviewing them.

Filing Status for Taxpayers

The following filing status descriptions were provided by bankrate.com:

Married Filing Jointly If you are married, you can file a joint return with your spouse. If your spouse died during the tax year, you are still able to file a joint return for that year.

Qualified Widow(er) You qualify for this status if your spouse died during the previous tax year (not the current tax year) and you and your spouse filed a joint tax return in the year immediately prior to their death. You are also required to have at least one dependent child or stepchild for whom you are the primary provider.

Single If you are divorced, legally separated, or unmarried as of the last day of the year you should use this status.

Head of Household This is the status for unmarried individuals that pay for more than half of the cost to keep up a home. This home needs to be the main home for the income tax filer and at least one qualifying relative. You can also choose this status if you are married, but didn't live with your spouse at any time during the last six months of the year. You also need to provide more than half of the cost to keep up your home and have at least one dependent child living with you.

Married Filing Separately This is also a filing option if you are married, but want to file your return independently instead of with your spouse. You might choose this option instead. Contact your CPA or tax accountant to determine if this option is more cost efficient. In the article "Married Filing Separately or Jointly: Which Tax Status Is Right for You?" by Money Crashers on March 13, 2012 on USAToday.com it states some areas that may make the difference:

1. **Income Differences and Investment Accounts** - Certain tax-deferred or tax-exempt investment accounts, such as Roth IRAs, carry contribution limits for individuals whose adjusted gross income falls above specified limits.

2. **Unreimbursed Medical Expenses** - Non-reimbursed medical expenses are any health care-related payments that have not been covered by an insurance company or similar institution.

3. **Miscellaneous and Business Deductions**- Miscellaneous and personal business deductions can only be claimed if they exceed 2 percent of the filer's income.

4. **Uninsured Property Losses** -Uninsured property losses work much the same way as non-reimbursed medical expenses for tax deduction purposes. The IRS allows individuals to deduct property loss expenses, such as roof damage not covered by insurance, as long as they exceed 10 percent of the filer's adjusted gross income.

Do You Know Your Tax Bracket?

Knowing your income tax rate can help you calculate your tax liability for unexpected income, retirement planning, or investment income. This calculator helps you estimate your average tax rate for 2012, your 2012 tax bracket, and your marginal tax rate for the 2012 tax year.

Single Taxpayers:

If Taxable Income Is:	The Tax Is:
Not over $9,075	10% of the taxable income
Over $9,075 but not over $36,900	$907.50 plus 15% of the excess over $9,075
Over $36,900 but not over $89,350	$5,081.25 plus 25% of the excess over $36,900
Over $89,350 but not over $186,350	$18,193.75 plus 28% of the excess over $89,350
Over $186,350 but not over $405,100	$45,353.75 plus 33% of the excess over $186,350
Over $405,100 but not over $406,750	$117,541.25 plus 35% of the excess over $405,100
Over $406,750	$118,188.75 plus 39.6% of the excess over $406,750

Married Filing Jointly and Surviving Spouses:

If Taxable Income Is:	The Tax Is:
Not over $18,150	10% of the taxable income
Over $18,150 but not over $73,800	$1,815 plus 15% of the excess over $18,150
Over $73,800 but not over $148,850	$10,162.50 plus 25% of the excess over $73,800
Over $148,850 but not over $226,850	$28,925 plus 28% of the excess over $148,850
Over $226,850 but not over $405,100	$50,765 plus 33% of the excess over $226,850
Over $405,100 but not over $457,600	$109,587.50 plus 35% of the excess over $405,100
Over $457,600	$127,962.50 plus 39.6% of the excess over $457,600

Head of Household:

If Taxable Income Is:	The Tax Is:
Not over $12,950	10% of the taxable income
Over $12,950 but not over $49,400	$1,295 plus 15% of the excess over $12,950
Over $49,400 but not over $127,550	$6,762.50 plus 25% of the excess over $49,400
Over $127,550 but not over $206,600	$26,300 plus 28% of the excess over $127,550
Over $206,600 but not over $405,100	$48,434 plus 33% of the excess over $206,600
Over $405,100 but not over $432,200	$113,939 plus 35% of the excess over $405,100
Over $432,200	$123,424 plus 39.6% of the excess over $432,200

Married Filing Separately:

If Taxable Income Is:	The Tax Is:
Not over $9,075	10% of the taxable income
Over $9,075 but not over $36,900	$907.50 plus 15% of the excess over $9,075
Over $36,900 but not over $74,425	$5,081.25 plus 25% of the excess over $36,900
Over $74,425 but not over $113,425	$14,462.50 plus 28% of the excess over $74,425
Over $113,425 but not over $202,550	$25,382.50 plus 33% of the excess over $113,425
Over $202,550 but not over $228,800	$54,793.75 plus 35% of the excess over $202,550
Over $228,800	$63,981.25 plus 39.6% of the excess over $228,800

Irs.gov states that the standard deduction rises to $6,200 for single taxpayers and married taxpayers filing separately. The standard deduction is $12,400 for married couples filing jointly and $9,100 for heads of household. Here's how those rates compare to 2013:

Filing Status	2014	2013
Single	$6,200	$6,100
Head of Household	$9,100	$8,950
Married Filing Jointly	$12,400	$12,200
Married Filing Separately	$6,200	$6,100

The IRS says 122 million taxpayers filed on line for free on irs.gov by either free file or IRS e-file. Visit www.irs.gov to see the filing date for your federal taxes, as filing late can cause you to incur late fees, interest, and other penalties. Efile.com stated that nearly 77 percent of taxpayers had their refunds direct deposited, to receive refunds faster. It doesn't matter if you can't file till mid-February because you don't have all your documentation in order; the tax deadline is still April 15th. This information is subject to change. Each year visit www.irs.gov to verify the tax filing deadline and when taxes can be filed.

If you ever want to determine your yearly tax liability, go to www.irs.gov and use their withholding calculator. You'll need your most recent pay stubs and income tax return. If you don't have this info, you can estimate the numbers; however, your results won't be as accurate as they would be if you were using actual data and not estimations. The calculated results will let you know what amounts should be held through your payroll. It will gauge if you are on track to break even or if you need to increase the amount you're withholding to ensure you don't have a tax liability at the end of the year.

As I stated earlier, most taxpayers only know what their income and deductions were for the prior year and are unaware of what tax credits, advantages, and government granted deductions are available to the average taxpayer. Below is a list of some of these items. Make sure you keep up with all your tax forms throughout the year to ensure you maximize your tax advantages.

Deductions vs. Credits

Deductions

1. Alimony Paid Tax Deduction

2. Self Employed SEP, SIMPLE, Retirement Plan Deduction

3. IRA Deduction

4. Educator Expenses Deduction

5. Tuition and Fees Deduction for College Expenses

6. Student Loan Interest Deduction

7. Health Savings Account Deduction

8. Moving Expenses Deduction

Credits

1. Earned Income Tax Credit

2. Education Credits

3. Child and Dependent Care Credit

4. Adoption Credit

5. Health Coverage Tax Credit

Saver's Credit

All deductions and credits and their descriptions can be found at www.irs.gov. You can also find dependent and exemptions details on this site.

Important Tax Tips

1. Visit irs.gov and review Publication 1 – Rights as a Taxpayer and Publication 17- Federal Income Tax Guide to get all taxpayer updates

2. If you have specific tax questions, visit irs.gov and chat with an interactive tax consultant or click on the IRS tax map to have questions answered

3. Gather all your tax documents including W-2s,1099-MISC, and any other related document before filing your yearly taxes (If you forget documents you could receive financial penalties or flag your return for an IRS audit)

4. Use e-file or free file at irs.gov to file your taxes if your adjusted gross income (AGI) is $57,000 or less.

5. If you are unable to use the resources on irs.gov to file your taxes, locate local non-profits or churches that allow you to file your taxes at no cost

6. Be sure to file your federal, state, and local taxes annually before the April 15th deadline, or file for an extension at irs.gov with Form 4868

7. To receive your refund faster, select the direct deposit option and you'll receive your tax refund within twenty-one days

8. Track all the charitable contributions you made throughout the year including donations made to the Salvation Army, Goodwill, non-profit organizations, etc.

9. File all your unfiled taxes and contact the IRS to make installment arrangements if you have a tax debt

Owing the IRS can be a scary thing. Uncle Sam is serious about his money. You've heard of A-list celebrities, politicians, and athletes going to prison for tax evasion. Chances are, you probably don't owe the IRS as much as any of those guys or gals, but irrespective of the amount, pay what you owe. Going to jail is probably the harshest punishment; however, there are other lesser but still stressful consequences including driver license suspensions and wage and bank garnishments. If you do owe the IRS or have not filed your taxes, avoiding the issue will only make it worse. Contact the IRS today and make arrangements. They will work with you and it's often not as bad as you think. Trust me—better you reach out to them than they reach out to you.

Installment Agreements

If you are unable to pay your outstanding tax liability in full, you can establish an installment agreement with the IRS, which will stop interest and other fees from accruing.

I Recommend You Do the Following Before Entering into an Agreement:

- File all required tax returns

- Consider other sources (loan or credit card) to pay your tax debt in full to save money

- Determine the largest monthly payment you can make ($25 minimum)

- Know that your future refunds will be applied to your tax debt until it is paid in full

Agreement Application Fees:

- $52 for a direct debit agreement

- $105 for a standard agreement or payroll deduction agreement

- $43 if your income is below a certain level.

Now, As Far As Applying Goes:

If you owe $50,000 or less in combined individual income tax, penalties and interest, complete and mail Form 9465, Installment Agreement Request at irs.gov. If you owe more than $50,000, you will also need to complete Form 433-F, Collection Information Statement.

Avoiding Default

To avoid defaulting on your agreement:

* Pay at least your minimum monthly payment

* Have it automatically deducted from your bank account to avoid missing the payment due date

* Include your name, address, social security number, daytime phone number, tax year, and tax return type on your payment

* File all future required tax returns on a timely basis

* Pay all taxes you owe in full and on time (contact the IRS to change your existing agreement if you cannot);

* Continue to make all scheduled payments even if your refund is applied to your account balance

* Ensure your statement is sent to the correct address. Contact the IRS if you move or complete and mail Form 8822, Change of Address.

I have met with individuals who have years of unfiled taxes and most of the time the reason they haven't filed is based on their fear of how much they might owe and they aren't aware of their options to initiate an installment agreement.

Benefits of filing outstanding tax returns:

Avoid Interest and Penalties

File your past due return and pay now to limit interest charges and late payment penalties.

Claim a Refund

You risk losing your refund if you don't file your return. If you are due a refund for withholding or estimated taxes, you must file your return to claim it within three years of the return due date. The same rule applies to a right to claim tax credits such as the Earned Income Credit.

The IRS holds income tax refunds in cases where their records show that one or more income tax returns are past due. The IRS holds them until they get the past due return or receive an acceptable reason for not filing a past due return.

Protect Social Security Benefits

If you are self-employed and do not file your federal income tax return, any self-employment income you earned will not be reported to the Social Security Administration and you will not receive credits toward Social Security retirement or disability benefits.

Avoid Issues Obtaining Loans

Loan approvals may be delayed if you don't file your return. Copies of filed tax returns must be submitted to financial institutions, mortgage lenders/brokers, etc., whenever you want to buy or refinance a home, get a loan for a business, or apply for federal aid for higher education.

If You Owe More Than You Can Pay

If you cannot pay what you owe, you can request an additional 60-120 days to pay your account in full through the Online Payment Agreement application or by calling 800-829-1040; no user fee will be charged. If you need more time to pay, you can request an installment agreement or you may qualify for an offer in compromise.

Substitute Return

If you fail to file, the IRS will file a substitute return for you. If IRS files a substitute return, it is still in your best interest to file your own tax return to take advantage of any exemptions, credits, and deductions you are entitled to receive. The IRS will generally adjust your account to reflect the correct figures.

Collection and Enforcement Actions

The return prepared for you or tax assessment will lead to a tax bill, which, if unpaid, will trigger the collection process. This can include such actions as a levy on your wages or bank account or the filing of a notice of a federal tax lien.

If you repeatedly do not file, you could be subject to additional enforcement measures, such as additional penalties and/or criminal prosecution.

Already Filed Your Past Due Return

If you received a notice, you should send a copy of the past due return to the indicated address. It takes approximately six weeks for the IRS to process an accurately completed past due tax return. Keep original copies of your tax returns.

Ways to Contact the IRS

www.irs.gov

For filing help, call 1-800-829-1040 or 1-800-829-4059 for TTY/ TDD. If you need income information to help prepare a past due return, call the toll-free number at 1-866-681-4271, or contact your employer or payer.

Get online tax forms and instructions to file your past due return, or order them by calling 1-800-Tax-Form (1-800-829-3676) or 1-800-829-4059 for TTY/TDD.

7

COMMUNITY IMPACT

Financial Institutions

On the first day of each week, you should each put aside a portion of the money you have earned. Don't wait until I get there and then try to collect it all at once.
(1 Corinthians 16:2 NLT)

According to Investopedia, a financial institution is an establishment that focuses on dealing with financial transactions, such as investments, loans, and deposits. Conventionally, financial institutions are composed of organizations such as banks, trust companies, insurance companies, and investment dealers. Most financial institutions are regulated by the government.

Understand that there are three major types of financial institutions:

1. **Depositary Institutions**: Deposit-taking institutions that accept and manage deposits and make loans, including banks, building societies, credit unions, trust companies, and mortgage loan companies (Faith Community United Credit Union, Fifth Third Bank, PNC, Huntington Bank)

2. **Contractual Institutions** : Insurance companies and pension funds (New York Life, Prudential, The Government Pension Fund of Norway)

3. **Investment Institutes**: Investment Banks, underwriters, brokerage firms (Morgan Stanley, Edward Jones, E*Trade)

The average person goes to their local financial institution just to cash their check and make deposits every Friday, or pay their house note or car loan at the beginning of the month. It's likely that very few of us know, get to know, or have a relationship with the persons who work at that specific location. We may have a particular teller whom we like because she always smiles and waits patiently when we have to fill out our withdrawal slip at the window, but we rarely really establish a relationship with the people at our local bank. Well, after today your assignment is to go and introduce yourself to the branch manager. When you do, get a business card with their contact info too so that the next time you have a question about your account, you're calling him or her, and not the 1-800 customer service number. (Thanks, Sharron Murphy-Williams).

Earlier in the book I discussed The Power of Five and the importance of relationships, and I'll say again, it's not only important who you know; it's also who knows you. While you're in the branch, browse the brochures and learn about products and services offered. Know what your financial institution can provide before you need it. Be an informed and equipped consumer, not an ignorant buyer.

Always remember that these institutions are in business to turn a profit for shareholders and/or members. Below are some of the items you need to consider when determining where you want to put your money. If you have to park your money somewhere, make an educated decision. I am trying to position you to have more savings than what is under the mattress, in your pocket, or in that jar on the counter. Change your habits increase your wealth.

How did you choose your current bank or credit union? It's not difficult, but it is important.

Things to Evaluate:

1. Level of technology offered

   a. Do they have a user-friendly app that you can conveniently access from your smartphone or tablet?

b. What about online banking? How simple is it to logon to check your account, balance, or update your profile information?

2. Ability to apply for a loan or credit product via website

3. Ability to pay bills online

4. Fees for accounts and services

5. Interest rate offered on savings and loan products (Credit unions are usually more competitive)

6. Locations and extended hours (Do they have a branch near your home and job? Are they open weekends or evenings?)

7. Friendly staff and service

8. Community involvement (What programs do they offer to the community?)

These are just a few of questions you can ask. Feel free to add to this checklist anything that would make you feel more comfortable with determining whether or not a particular financial institution is the one for you. Treat this relationship like you would the one you have with your job—something you don't want to change every few years.

I stated earlier that I have been banking with the same bank since I was thirteen years old. Of course, management and staff have changed and as a matter-of-fact, the branch where I actually opened my account closed its doors at the end of 2013, which brings me to my next bit of advice: diversify. You'll hear this term come up in investing a lot, but it's applicable in this context as well. You don't necessarily want all your money tied up in one bank. In my experience, banks don't close branches frequently, but, it does happen, so personally, I do business with a bank and a credit union.

When choosing a financial institution to conduct your banking, you may want to also consider a credit union. On www.creditunions.com they positively stated as of September 2013, the nation's 6,753 credit unions held $1.07 trillion in assets, up 4.3 percent from the previous September. They are owned by their members and are truly community based.

Shameless plug, I currently sit as the president of the Board of Directors for Faith Community United Credit Union (FCUCU), a CDFI (Community Development Financial Institution), located in Cleveland, Ohio. If you are a Cuyahoga County resident visit our website at www.faithcommcu.com or visit us in person at:

Faith Community United Credit Union
3550 East 93rd Street (near 93rd and Union)
Cleveland, Ohio 44105-1644
Phone: (216) 271-7111

It is the largest African-American credit union in the state of Ohio. It was founded in 1952 by Rita Haynes, who is one of my mentors and the current CEO emeritus, and others. Her husband, James Haynes, is a successful businessman who has also been a mentor to me, always willing to assist me in overcoming any obstacles and pursuing my vision. It was established with the purpose of attempting to address the financial disparities in the black community at that time and continues to service and operate with this same purpose now over six decades later. A group of people came together in the basement of a Cleveland church, put their money together, and FCUCU was born, which since has experienced a name and location change. To learn more and to view financial statistics about credit unions visit the CUNA (Credit Union National Association) website at www.cuna.org.

I am aware that most people reading this can't do their banking in Cleveland. The point is to find a credit union in your area with vision and a proven track record of working hard to develop the people in the community where it exists. Take some time to research credit unions and learn more about the movement of these institutions.

For those of you who have ninety-nine problems but money isn't one, you may want to consider opening a deposit account at your local community credit union. The more deposits coming in, the more they can lend to the community. When local credit unions have the resources to fund civil causes, everyone benefits. They can help qualified, low-income families become home owners, which contributes to neighborhood pride and stability; they can assist entrepreneurs with cash to start a business or take their business to another level, again, enabling those individuals to put money back into the community and support the local economy as well.

Review the features and benefits of credit unions and banks and you'll find that there are a number of differences between the two. Some of the differences could save you money and time. One of the key differences between these two institutions is the ownership and how they function. Credit unions appear to provide more personalized service to account holders than banks. In most cases, credit unions are designed to serve the underbanked or underserved because of their geographical location in communities where there are limited bank branches and limited bank products to fit their needs.

For example, FCUCU has a product called *Wheelz* where it allows you the ability to purchase an affordable car with a low credit score for the purposes of transportation to and from work, while you work to build your score and increase your level of responsibility. The interest rate will be higher than a normal interest rate due to the exceptions and risk factors. But it gives an individual who has a good work ethic and income a second chance to build their financial credibility.

Another example is the Score Builder program. This product was created to help individuals with low credit scores rebuild their score by paying off a debt of up to $5,000.00. In many cases, people have just a few bills weighing down their score: old medical, utility, or credit card bills. Once all collections and outstanding bills are consolidated and paid for, your credit score will rise and you'll have an affordable payment. This program allows people who want to consider purchasing a new vehicle or home the ability to raise their score and receive a competitive interest rate. So, if used properly, it will give someone a new opportunity and create a cycle of financial responsibility. You won't find products like these in many corporately-owned banks.

Banks vs. Credit Unions

Ownership

Banks' primary objective is to turn a profit for the owners, who are the investors of the bank. Banks will function and operate in the best interest of the owners to make sure they are realizing a return on the money they have put forward in the operation of the bank. Anyone who has an account with a credit union is actually a part owner because credit union members are the owners. When a credit union makes a profit it is returned to the members in the form of a dividend.

Profit/Non-Profit

Banks tend to charge significantly more in fees and penalties for services and customer errors that by comparison, credit unions don't. Credit unions have fewer fees in general and better interest rates. Accounts you establish at credit unions save you money. Banks are for-profit organizations, and credit unions are non-profit organizations. (That should tell you something about the thinking, approach, and purpose of banks and credit unions). This accounts for the contrast in rates and fees between the two.

Location

From a convenience standpoint, credit unions have a limited amount of locations (usually only one), whereas, most banks have multiple branches throughout the city. If you need to stop in your bank and speak to a representative, a branch office is likely within a few miles or so of wherever you are. Credit unions have fewer branches than traditional banks and customers may have trouble accessing a branch or avoiding ATM fees.

Insured

Banks' money is insured by the Federal Deposit Insurance Corporation (FDIC). Each depositor per account is insured up to $250,000 as of December 31, 2009. Visit www.fdic.gov to verify updated information. Some people believe credit unions don't offer any type of insurance, but they are federally insured by the National Credit Union Administration (NCUA) which provides the same amount of coverage as FDIC. Visit www.nuca.gov. For more information. Some credit unions are privately insured by ASI (American Share Insurance). For more details visit www.americanshare.com.

Members

In some cases to join, you may have to be a part of a particular group such as an employee of a certain company, a firefighter, or a teacher. Certain credit unions restrict membership to customers who meet a certain profile. Some credit unions offer membership to people living in a specific town or city. Thankfully, there are others that are simply community-based so everyone is welcome, like FCUCU. On the other hand, when you get ready to open an account at a bank, you don't have to worry about exclusivity clauses—anyone is accepted with no membership requirements. Before you go off gallivanting to your local credit union, call to see if you qualify for membership.

Products/Services

Banks have more products and services to offer than credit unions. They have various mortgage, business, auto, and personal loans, and a range of credit card, IRA, and CDs. Banks are to credit unions what buffets are to cafes. If you check with some of the larger credit unions, you will find that they too have a diverse range of products to offer, but still not as many as banks. This is another reason why I have relationships with both a bank and a credit union.

Fees

Many credit unions offer free checking accounts, meaning customers do not have to pay a monthly maintenance fee. Similar to banks, credit unions charge fees for overdrafts, returned checks, and ATM withdrawals; however, the fees credit unions charge are typically smaller. According to Bankrate.com, as of 2010, the average fee for an overdraft at a traditional bank is $29.58, while that same overdraft would cost $24.88 at a credit union.

Interest Rates

Typically, credit unions offer a better interest rate on the same financial products offered by banks. For example, Neighborhood Residential Community Credit Union members can earn higher interest rates on savings accounts and CDs or open an auto loan with a lower interest rate than what they'd get at National Nationwide US Corporate Bank. This can save the customer money over the course of their banking relationship.

Balance Requirements

Many traditional banks have a minimum opening balance requirement for new checking accounts. A study by Bankrate.com shows that as of 2010, twenty-seven of the fifty credit unions they polled for the study do not have an opening balance requirement. For checking accounts, most traditional banks also require that the customer keep a minimum balance in the account to avoid fees. The same Bankrate.com study showed that forty-one out of the fifty credit unions polled did not require a minimum balance for checking accounts.

Considerations

The biggest disadvantage of using a bank versus a credit union is that a bank is a profit corporation. Their chief interest is to make sure having you as a customer benefits their owners, and in some cases, they do not consider what is in the customer's best interest. Additionally, banks may be reluctant to offer you the personalized service that you need because you are only a customer and not a shareholder. A bank's primary obligation is to its shareholders.

Don't get me wrong here. I'm not a bank basher. I just want to make sure you aware of your options. Some banks are more committed to the community than others. Also, there are banks with branches that have incredible customer service and staff that are willing to help you accomplish your personal finance goals. What it boils down to then, is what your goals are, who can best help you achieve them, and how they're going to work with you to accomplish them.

The key is diversification. I have products at both. Both have been beneficial to assisting my family accomplish our goals. Because I did my homework, I have great relationships with bank CEOs and VPs, and the same with credit unions. Both credit unions and banks have assisted with various projects that impacted our local community.

Do your homework! Let's also agree from this day forward you will be a great customer and you will not change your bank account each month, due to your lack of taking financial responsibility. Stop closing accounts because of extreme overdrafts and payday loans draining your account weekly. Keep better records!

8

READ THE MENU

Products Offered

No one can serve two masters. For you will hate one and love the other; you will be devoted to one and despise the other. You cannot serve both God and money. (Matthew 6:24 NLT)

In the chapter previous, I discussed the differences between credit unions and banks. Use the criteria I provided to assist you with finding a financial institution that meets your daily needs. Learn what products your financial institution offers and how to make them work for you. I will continue to reiterate the importance of educating yourself so you can converse knowledgeably when it comes to your finances. You are less likely to be taken advantage of when you are well read and familiar with your options. The website below will assist you with finding an institution that meets your needs.

www.findabetterbank.com

When you visit the site, you'll find questions concerning which bank services and products are important to you. (I've listed some of them below). Your answers will ensure that you're matched with the financial institution best suited to meet your needs, while allowing you to compare competitors, apples to apples.

1. Overdraft protection

2. Interest on balances

3. Online bill pay services

4. Twenty-four hour automated telephone banking

5. Mobile banking

6. Deposits with mobile phone

7. Email and text alerts

8. ATM access

9. Loan and credit products

10. Loans and mortgages

11. Stock and mutual fund trading

12. Retirement planning services

13. Small business services

14. Safe deposit box rental

Take some time to visit various financial institutions until you feel comfortable with a particular branch (or branches). Use the three C's —chemistry, competency, and character. For example, I was in Baton Rouge visiting my client, Rose Hill Church, and we did a tour of banks. We planned to visit three institutions. We didn't make any appointments, but we did call ahead to make sure the banker was in the office so that the trip wouldn't be a waste of time. We began by informing the banker of what our needs were. However, after every statement she said, "We don't offer that," or "That's impossible." And she made us feel even more uncomfortable by giving us excuses as to why she was unprepared when she couldn't answer basic questions about the details of their services and products. Remember, we were asking about products that she sells every day.

We arrived at the second bank and the service was absolutely phenomenal. The banker, who was also the Vice President of

Community Affairs, said that if we came back in an hour, she would have her entire team prepared to meet with us. When we returned, there were four or five bankers from every area of business banking seated around a conference table waiting for us. The VP remembered my client from over a year ago, and not only did he remember him, but he recalled small details about my client's ministry and family. We were so at ease in their presence that we felt like there were no other options. Trust me; you will know when there is a fit.

They were well prepared for our meeting, and so were we. When it was over, all of our questions were answered. The only thing left to do was to provide additional info and get a proposal in return to ensure pricing was competitive. Though that meeting went well, I still had to compare the proposal with another institution's to ensure we received fair pricing. I can't say this enough: financial institutions are in business to make money. Do your due diligence.

To find the best rates when purchasing a mortgage, insurance policy, or a vehicle, or opening an investment, checking, or savings account, or applying for credit cards visit www.bankrate.com. Remember, you have made the commitment to be smart about your finances. Now that you have worked on repairing or establishing your credit you want to ensure you receive the best rates. Challenge the financial institution you have a relationship with to always give you the best rate on their products. There are hundreds (if not thousands) of different offers out there. Whenever possible, you'll want to do business with your credit union or bank. But, if some other bank is offering a lower interest rate on a loan or a higher interest rate on a CD, it may make sense to go with that offer.

Two of the most common questions you get when you first step foot onto a car lot is "How much can you put down?" Or, "How much can you afford each month?" The salesman never asks how much you want to spend on a car or what your credit score is. I think they do this to find out what they'll have to work with based on your answers once they pull your credit report. They can now inform the bank of how much skin you are putting in the game based on the amount of your down payment. Every bit of advice I offer you throughout this book is to make sure you are in the driver's seat in any purchase you make moving forward.

TimeValue Software (www.tcalc.timevalue.com) offers financial calculators to help you determine what you can afford to spend when buying a car or securing a mortgage. They also offer tools for debt cancellation and guidelines for how to meet your investment goals. Visit the site and take advantage of the insight you gain before you make a major purchase or request a loan of some sort. By doing so, you will know what the preapproval amount for your mortgage should be before you apply. Remember, don't get excited when the bank tells you "yes." Know what you can afford so you have no regrets after your purchase. The new car and new house smell wear off quick.

Now, let's talk about some of the most common products out there. Almost all financial institutions offer checking, savings, and money market accounts, as well as certificates of deposit (CDs) to house your money.

A few items to verify when opening an account:

FDIC

If you have over $250,000 in the bank, you may want to make sure your money is properly insured by the FDIC beyond that figure. The FDIC suggests that you visit www.FDIC.gov/EDIE and use the Electronic Deposit Insurance Estimator to calculate your coverage. If you prefer to speak to someone, you can call 1-877-ASK-FDIC.

Chex Systems

Have you bounced checks or overdrawn your account and not paid the bank whatever the charges and associated fees were? There are people who have done this with several financial institutions. If you have, then you know this financial hiccup will pose some problems when you try to move forward and get an account. If you haven't… well, don't. Every institution has different rules, but if you do happen to be one of the people, who, for some reason or another, overdrew your account or bounced checks and didn't pay back what you owed, you're probably flagged in Chex Systems.

So what is Chex Systems? Consumerdebit.com defines Chex Systems, Inc. as a network comprised of member financial institutions that regularly contribute information on closed checking and savings accounts. Chex Systems shares this information among its member institutions to help them assess the risk of opening new accounts. Chex Systems does not make account opening decisions for its members. Those decisions are made by the member institutions based on their internal policies. Some institutions will allow you to open a savings account while in Chex Systems, but most will make you show proof that past charges have been paid.

To receive a copy of your **Consumer (Chex Systems) Report:**

Call 1-800-428-9623 or go to www.consumerdebit.com.

To order by mail:

Print and complete the order form found at the website (available in printable format)

Mail to:
Chex Systems, Inc.

Attn: Consumer Relations
7805 Hudson Road, Suite 100
Woodbury, Minnesota 55125

To order by fax:

Fax to 602.659.2197

If you've had trouble balancing your bank account, obtain your report and pay your past debts; everyone needs a bank account. Many employers even make it mandatory for you to have direct deposit. And when you decide it's time to purchase your home or car and you need a loan, you want to go to your bank. Remember the importance of relationships.

Types of Bank Accounts

Investorguide.com breaks down the five types of bank accounts offered at financial institutions.

Savings Accounts

Most institutions offer Student/Minor savings accounts for children under the age of eighteen. I encourage you to start saving for your child as soon as possible. Having their own account will teach them how to manage money and how to be responsible with their finances. Also, because of compound interest (interest that builds on both the principal and interest that has accumulated over a certain period of time), the earlier they start the better off they will be. A great habit to start is using your ledger book to keep record of all transactions. Most people get these savings ledger books when opening their accounts and never use them to keep up with their transactions.

And then there are basic savings accounts, which pay you a minimal interest rate. You can't write checks from a savings account, but if you are trying to stabilize your finances you should start with a savings account. By doing so, you'll learn how to maintain an account and keep good records. You can't overdraw a savings account, so you needn't worry about overdraft fees.

If you're pretty stable when it comes to balancing your books and maintaining your accounts, then you should have two savings accounts: one that is your emergency or rainy day fund, and another that we'll call your "Can't-Touch-This" account. I have a rule called the Twenty-Mile Rule. Your "Can't-Touch-This" savings account should be at least twenty miles from your home or job.

Most people today are dealing with the issues of attempting to save each pay period, but continue to use their savings to cover overdraft fees being applied to their checking account, which forces them to deplete the savings they have worked hard to accumulate. They feel like they have been saving forever but have nothing to show for it.

I recommend every couple or individual I meet with to apply my Twenty-Mile Rule, especially if they have no savings and are trying to establish their emergency fund of $1,000 (that is the recommended minimum by most financial gurus).

After you accumulate your first thousand dollars, next you should try to save at least three to six months of your monthly expenses. Don't give yourself too much credit. Remember, every January 1st you make a resolution to save some money, but when December 31st comes you are waiting on your W-2s so you can e-file your taxes, to receive your refund, to start your savings; that usually lasts you till end of March or early April. By that time you have purchased everything you felt you deserved or that you wanted, and have no savings left.

Don't just think about it, let's do it! If your account is twenty miles away, more than likely you will think through your purchases a little more thoroughly. You'll weigh your needs versus wants before you spend fifty bucks to fill up the tank and make that trip. My wife and I have an account in another city twenty miles away and she has been there less than five times in as many years. We have a portion of our payroll automatically deducted and transferred into that account and a portion into our rainy day account. Try it.

Utilize the following chart as a simple way to save for the first year. I'm quite sure you have seen it floating around the Internet. You have to make your savings a priority. Have your spouse join you and you both do it individually, so the savings amount doubles. If you can save more, then do so. Make it a fifty-two week challenge that your entire immediate family is aware of. Once the excitement begins and you get going you will begin depositing double and triple the amount that the chart says per week. Most people enjoy watching their numbers grow.

Remember, it is important that you have a rainy day savings account and the Can't-Touch-This account. The rainy day, short-term account can be at the bank where your checking account is at and can even be attached to your checking account to ensure you avoid overdrafts fees that could possibly occur. This account should always have at least $1000 available. The Can't-Touch-This account should be at an institution that adheres to the Twenty-Mile Rule. This is your true emergency fund, long-term, for items like job loss, major car or house repairs, or if experiencing major illnesses. The Can't-Touch-This fund should at the minimum have at least three to six months of your monthly expenses. That's a starting goal to aim for.

Basic Checking Accounts

A basic checking account allows you to write checks (with some institutions limiting how many you can write), make purchases with a debit card, and withdraw money from ATMs. Some institutions offer free checking account services and/or lower fees. In most cases, this account doesn't offer interest or any extra features.

Interest-Bearing Checking Accounts

Unlike a basic checking account this account offers more features, but with additional costs. Also unlike a basic checking account, you are usually able to write an unlimited number of checks. Checking accounts that pay interest are sometimes referred to as negotiable order of withdrawal (NOW) accounts. Your interest rate will depend on the balance you maintain in the account.

Money Market Deposit Accounts (MMDAs)

These accounts offer you a higher interest rate due to the bank investing it in commercial paper, Treasury Bills, or CDs. This account typically requires a higher balance. They provide limited check-writing privileges (three transfers by check, and six total transfers per month), and often impose a service fee if your balance falls below a certain level.

Certificates of Deposit (CDs)

Invest Guide calls these "time deposits" because the account holder has agreed to keep the money in the account for a specified amount of time, anywhere from three months to six years. This account doesn't allow for withdrawals. The account holder is rewarded with a higher interest rate, with the rate increasing as the duration increases. There is a substantial penalty for early withdrawal so don't select this option if you think you might need the money before the time period is over (the "maturity date"). These common short-term investment products are becoming increasingly popular due to interest rates being so low with money market and savings accounts.

Types of Bank Loans

Secured Loans

Secured loans are loans that are guaranteed by property. Examples are auto, mortgage, and home equity loans. With this type of loan, you can get a fixed or variable rate. With a fixed rate, the rate remains the same for the entire loan and the payment remains the same. With fixed rates, it's easy to budget because you know exactly how much you'll be paying every month. With a variable rate, the rate will fluctuate, thus so will the payment.

For example, when you get a 5/1 adjustable rate mortgage (ARM) loan, the rate remains fixed for five years and adjusts once those years are up or until you pay off or refinance.

I always advise my clients to get a fixed rate. The housing market is volatile, and it is often hard to predict, making it difficult to accurately budget for your payment when you have an ARM. If rates rise tremendously, it could force you to default on the loan and lose the asset due to your inability to cover the payment. These types of loans range anywhere from one to thirty years based on the asset.

Auto Loan

An auto loan is a secured loan where the collateral is the vehicle. This type of loan payment option ranges from twelve to eighty-four months. It's offered by banks and credit unions and also by the dealerships. I would advise you to do your research online at www.bankrate.com or on your financial institution's website to see where you can land the best deal. In some cases, the dealership advertises deals like two thousand dollars cash back or a zero percent loan. Of course, the bank will never offer you a zero percent loan. With the cash back option, use the loan calculator to figure out based on your down payment, interest rate, cost of the vehicle, trade-in value and the payment terms the interest you will pay for the life of the loan. At that point you can determine if you would rather take the cash back option. Use www.edmunds.com to calculate the monthly payment and interest payments for the life of the loan.

Types of Mortgage Loans

- **Fixed-Rate Mortgage Types**

The fixed-rate mortgage is the most common mortgage. The term can range from five to forty years based on the lending institution. These loans are amortized.   In the article "Private Mortgage Insurance (PMI) – How to Avoid Paying It" by Kira Botkin, she states that PMI is usually applied when the loan-to-value is greater than 80 percent. This gives the mortgage lender insurance in case of a foreclosure and the home has to be sold at a discount.

- **FHA Loans – Federal Housing Administration**

www.fha.com

FHA mortgage loan types are insured by the government through mortgage insurance that is funded into the loan. This loan type is ideal for first-time home buyers because the down payment requirements are minimal and FICO scores do not matter or can be lower. Also, the buyer can assist with down payment costs. The

Mortgage Insurance Premium (MIP) can be removed when you refinance after twelve to twenty-four months.

- **VA Loans – Veterans Administration**

www.va.gov

This is a government loan that is available to veterans who have served in the U.S. Armed Services and, in certain cases, to spouses of deceased veterans. The requirements vary depending on the year of service and whether the discharge was honorable or dishonorable. The main benefit is the lack of need of a down payment. The loan is guaranteed by the Department of Veteran Affairs, but funded by a financial institution lender.

- **Interest-Only Mortgage Types**

This loan type allows borrowers the option to pay only interest on the loan. But the borrowers should always make a principal payment to increase the equity in their home by decreasing the principal balance. This is not a common option, nor do I advise you use this option. Most people create their bills based on their expenses. If that is the case, no principal will be paid. So, if you're in the same home for ten years, and you purchased it for $200,000 and you make these payments only, in ten years you will still owe $200,000.

Hybrid Types of Mortgage Loans

- **Option ARM Mortgage Types**

Option ARM loans are complicated. They are adjustable-rate mortgages, meaning the interest rate fluctuates periodically. Like the name implies, borrowers can choose from a variety of payment options. But, beware of the minimum payment option, which can result in negative amortization. This occurs whenever the loan payment for any period is less than the interest charged over that period so that the outstanding balance of the loan increases.

- **Combo/Piggyback Mortgage Loan Types**

This type of mortgage financing consists of two loans: a first mortgage and a second mortgage. The mortgages can be adjustable-rate mortgages or fixed-rate or a combination of the two. Borrowers take out two loans when the down payment is less than 20 percent to avoid paying private mortgage insurance.

- **Adjustable-Rate Mortgage Types**

ARMs come in many flavors, colors, and sizes. The interest rate fluctuates. It can move up or down monthly, semi-annually, annually, or remain fixed for a period of time before it adjusts.

Specialty Mortgage Loan Types

- **203K Mortgage Loans**

Like the 203K loan program. Realtor.com states that 203K loans are designated for houses that are damaged and in need of rehabilitation. The 203K covers not only the cost of the property but also the cost of necessary home repairs. Usually, the down payment requirement is low, and eligibility criteria more lenient than usual. Homeowners whose homes need improvement can also refinance with these loans. The FHA (Federal Housing Authority) has another program that provides funds to a borrower to fix up a home by rolling the funds into one loan. The dollar limits for repair work are lower on a Streamlined-K loan, but it requires less paperwork and is easier to obtain than a 203K.

- **Bridge/Swing Loans**

These types of mortgage loans are used when a seller has put a home on the market—but it has not yet sold—and the seller wants to borrow equity to buy another home. The seller's existing home is used as security for a bridge (also called swing) loan.

- **Equity Mortgage Loan Types**

Equity loans that can be utilized for home improvements and personal needs are equity mortgage loans.   This loan will be considered a second mortgage or in second position. Unless the home was paid in full, then it would be in first position. The loans can be adjustable, fixed, or a line of credit from which the borrower can draw funds as needed.

- **Reverse Mortgages**

Reverse mortgage are available to any person over the age of sixty-two who has equity in the home. Instead of making monthly payments to the lender, the lender makes monthly payments to the borrower for as long as the borrower resides in the home. The equity will decrease and the debt on the home will continue to increase. The interest rate can be fixed or adjustable. Get independent advice from a trusted advisor before taking out a reverse mortgage. Visit www.aarp.org and www.reversemortgage.com to get third-party counseling if considering this option. This loan is like no other so it can get confusing.

Home Equity Loan

A home equity loan is a loan with home as collateral: a loan by which the borrower's home is used as collateral, usually secondary to a first mortgage. When you decide to take the loan, if your home is has no current mortgage (paid in full), this loan will be the first lien. It has a fixed interest rate for a fixed period of time. In most cases, it's utilized to consolidate debt, education, purchase a car, home repairs, or additions or to take a vacation.

Home Equity Line of Credit (HELOC)

Webster's states that a home equity line of credit differs from an equity loan because the borrower is not advanced the entire sum up front, but uses a line of credit to borrow sums that total no more than the credit limit, similar to a credit card. HELOC funds can be borrowed during the "draw period" (typically five to twenty-five years). Repayment is of the amount drawn plus interest. A HELOC may have a minimum monthly payment requirement usually interest only payments. The full principal amount is due at the end of the draw period, either as a lump-sum balloon payment or according to a loan amortization schedule. The interest rate is usually variable. The interest rate is generally based on an index, such as the prime rate. This means that the interest rate can change over time.

HELOC is very popular in part because interest paid was and is typically deductible under federal and many state income tax laws; consult your CPA or tax accountant. This effectively reduced the cost of borrowing funds and offered an attractive tax incentive over traditional methods of borrowing, such as credit card debt. Another reason for the popularity of HELOC is flexibility, both in terms of borrowing and repaying on a schedule determined by the borrower. HELOC is considered a second mortgage unless the home is paid in full upon getting the loan.

Unsecured Loans

Loans that are based on your credit and have no collateral are unsecured loans. Personal/Signature loans are considered to be unsecured loans. These types of loans usually have higher interest rates and the terms range from one to six years. In most cases, these are utilized to build your credit. With an unsecured product, which has no tangible collateral attached like a home or car, it's just your signature. The loan will likely be granted at a higher interest rate. For example, with great credit you could pay 2 – 4 percent for a new car loan. With a signature or unsecured loan, it could possibly be seven – fourteen percent, depending on the institution. With the unsecured loan it puts the financial institution at a higher level of risk with no recourse or asset to retrieve in the event of possible default or non-payment on the loan.

Examples of unsecured loans are student loans and credit cards, all only needing your signature in order to acquire them.

Credit or Debit?

Who hasn't heard that question at the register? **Before we go any further, take all your cards out of your wallet or purse and write "See ID" on the back.** This will ensure that if your card is stolen the cashier will ask for ID or it may deter a thief from using the card out of fear of being caught. In most cases, both debit and credit cards are accepted at all the same places and both offer the same level of convenience. What are they and what are the differences? Bing's dictionary defines credit card as a card for deferring payment: a card issued by a bank or business that allows somebody to purchase goods and services and pay for them later, often with interest, based on your personal credit situation.

Bing's dictionary defines debit card as a card used for shopping without cash: a plastic card that the holder can use to pay for purchases, the money being transferred directly from the holder's bank account to the seller.

In other words, when you use a debit card, the money is taken directly from your bank account. When you use a credit card, the purchase is deducted from your line of credit, and you must pay that money back within a certain period (plus interest, most of the time).

When you make a purchase with a debit card, the funds in your account are put on hold or placed in a pending status until the transaction clears, usually within twenty-four to forty-eight hours, but sometimes may take a little longer depending on the merchant processing the transaction. If you use your PIN (Personal Identification Number) when making your purchase, you can also opt to get cash back over the amount of your purchase, saving you a trip to the ATM, but be careful with using your PIN. Some financial institutions will charge you fees when you do a PIN-assisted transaction.

On the other hand, when you make a purchase with a credit card, the amount of available credit you have will be reduced by the transaction amount. As with a debit card, the funds will still show as pending until the transaction settles. Some credit card companies take a few days to clear your transactions and the amount of your purchase is not always immediately deducted from your credit limit. This is why it's important that you track your transactions on your own and not depend on your online banking statement or some representative on the other end of a 1-800 number. I call that being a *pending player*; you really never know exactly what your true balance is. When you don't carefully monitor your card usage, you're more likely to incur overdraft fees and/or over-the-limit charges. Hopefully, you won't ever be anywhere near your credit limit because if you've been paying attention, you know that you need to keep your overall balance below 30 percent of your total limit anyhow.

The bank who issues you your credit card allows you to borrow (up to) a certain amount of money, and then they charge you interest on the portion of money you decide to use out of what they've loaned you. There is generally a grace period of approximately thirty days before interest is charged, which means that if you pay the entire balance off in thirty days, you won't owe interest. If you allow the balance to remain after the thirty-day period, you will be charged interest every month until your balance has reached zero.

Types of Cards

AmericanExpress.com shares information about the different kinds of cards that are available to consumers. Also, make sure you make copies of the front and back of all your cards when you receive them. This will help you if the card is ever lost or stolen. Also, put See ID in signature bar on the back of the card to ensure that the cashier asks with every transaction.

Low APR (Annual Percentage Rate)

Lower interest rates allow more of your monthly payment to be applied towards your principal balance. Always look for a card with the lowest interest rate possible.

Rewards Program

Cards of this type offer cash back on your purchases—sometimes 1 to 5 percent of purchase amounts—as well as points for hotel stays, airline tickets, and gasoline.

Secured Credit Card

This card is usually recommended when you have a low credit score or no score at all. With a secure credit card, you send your own money (a deposit) to the bank issuing the credit card, and they in turn provide you with a card you can use to build or establish your credit. The deposit you send can be fifty to one hundred percent of your limit. In terms of credit bureau reporting, it works the same as any other credit card; the company reports monthly to the three agencies.

Some banks will have you maintain a secured credit card for one year then transfer you to a basic credit card. Secured credit cards can be helpful for those with compromised credit, however, beware that these kinds of cards often have higher fees (including an application fee and annual fee) and interest rates higher than unsecured (or regular) credit cards.

Retail Card

A retail card is a card with a line of credit extended for a particular store, like Walmart for example. Many people get these cards to stores that they frequent. Retailers who offer their own store credit card often give coupons and rewards points to their cardholders to be used toward purchases made at that retailer. Some retailers even offer their own debit cards, where the card is linked to your checking account. Target offers just such a card (the REDcard) and even provides a 5 percent discount every time you use it. Be wary of retail credit cards too, though. They often come bridled with high interest rates irrespective of how good your credit score is.

Pre-Paid Card

A card that requires the user to load money for purchases is a pre-paid card. Once you spend whatever amount you've loaded, the card is empty and you have to load it again. Like the secured credit card, this card is popular for people in Chex Systems who don't have any credit or bad credit. The information can possibly stay in Chex Systems' records for five years.

Some retail stores use Chex Systems to verify and approve checks written by customers, so if your name is in Chex Systems, your checks will be denied until the issue is rectified. In some cases, if you write a bad check with no funds actually available, the retailer will place you on Chex Systems. The big difference is, this card will not help you build your credit, as your credit activity is not reported to the credit bureaus.

Charge Card

A charge card is a card that usually has no spending limit, but is due in full every thirty days. You don't have to worry about interest or finance charges with this kind of card for the most part, but it does typically carry an annual fee. (How else would the bank make money?) The term *charge* card is often used synonymously with *credit* card; however, there are distinct differences: credit cards have a limit, charge cards don't. Credit cards require you to only pay a minimum amount every month; charge cards require the full balance to be paid every month.

Business Credit Card

A business credit card is similar to a consumer credit card. Business owners can utilize it for business expenses. It helps with cash flow on a monthly basis due to you not having to pay the balance twenty-five to twenty-eight days later, and keeps you from having to pay for expenses with cash at the time of each transaction. These cards in some cases offer rewards. The biggest difference between a business card and a consumer card is the following:

- Use tax-id number vs. social security number to apply

- In some cases have to provide financial statements to qualify

- Receive quarterly analysis report with transactions

- In some cases higher limits are provided

- Usually paid in full on a monthly basis

Payday Loans

Investopedia defines a payday loan as a type of short-term borrowing where an individual borrows a small amount at a very high rate of interest. The borrower typically writes a post-dated check in the amount they wish to borrow plus a fee in exchange for cash.

How does the commercial go? "If you need to make a car repair or pay a bill before your next payday and you have a bank account and direct deposit, you are preapproved for a cash advance or payday loan today for $100-$1,500."

Under no circumstance do I want to see anyone get caught in this vicious cycle. If you do find yourself in a situation where you need money, and you have no one or nowhere to get it from, know that payday loans are only helpful the first time you get them. A payday loan is just a Band-Aid. Pay it back immediately and do not return to get another one the following week. And if you do have to get a payday loan, opt to go into the location instead of online; the fees are lower.

For example, if you visit Check 'n Go's website, an online cash advance for $250 will cost you 676.71 percent for a fourteen-day term, which equals $314.89. If you visit the store, the fees are 285.64 percent for a fourteen-day term for $250.00, which equals

$277.39. Make sure you only borrow what you can afford to pay back on your next pay day and still have some money left to get you to your next pay period. If you don't, you will get caught in a hard-to-untangle web that you'll find difficult to detach yourself from. Review the following chart to see the fees that you'll pay.

Fourteen-day Term, Online Loan Fees

	2 week	4 week	6 week	8 week	10 week	12 week	14 week
$300	$77	$155	$233	$311	$389	$467	$545
$400	$103	$206	$309	$412	$515	$618	$721
$500	$129	$258	$387	$516	$645	$774	$903
$600	$155	$310	$465	$620	$775	$930	$1085

In most cases, when I sit down with a couple who have payday loan troubles, they have multiple payday loans at one time. It only takes a few moments into the conversation to discover that their situation needs more than a quick fix. It's time to do a complete overhaul of their financial situation.

The ads are on the radio, television, the Internet, even in the mail. They're referred to as payday loans, cash advance loans, check advance loans, post-dated check loans, or deferred deposit loans. The Federal Trade Commission (FTC), the nation's consumer protection agency, says that regardless of their name, these small, short-term, high-rate loans by check cashers, finance companies, and others all come at a very high price.

Before you consider acquiring a cash advance consider the following:

1. Is the expense a need or a want?

2. Can you contact the creditor and get an extension?

3. Can you use a credit card, which has a lower rate of 10-19 percent vs. 250-678 percent?

4. Can you borrow money from a family member? (There is no interest).

5. Have you tried to get a short-term loan from your bank or credit union?

9

WISE CHOICES

—

Invest in Your Future

The rich rules over the poor, And the borrower becomes the lender's slave. (Proverbs 22:7 NASB)

Investing is an area that the average person avoids because they are unknowledgeable about it. It could be the fancy terms, the myriad products, or all those confusing symbols and letters running across the ticker at the bottom of news channels that intimidate people. But Wall Street is where your money can really work for you. It's in your best interest to get as familiar as possible with at least the basics of investment strategy and as you get more comfortable, challenge yourself to learn even more. Meet with a financial advisor to create a strategy that will assist with meeting your goals. Make investing a priority.

Like anything worth investing in, it should be also worth educating yourself in. At some point, we have to retire. After all, unless you're Benjamin Button, you're getting older every year and eventually you will no longer be able to (or want to) put in the kind of hours you can when you're between the ages of twenty-five and fifty-four, your prime working years. You've got to start thinking about what you're going to do when it's time for you to turn in the badge, sell your last home, or teach your last class.

You hear most people talk about what they're going to do when they retire; travel the world, relocate to a warmer climate or just even relax and golf every day. In order live that lifestyle it will come with a cost. That's why preparing for your retirement is imperative. Paying your house and all debt off, building your savings account, and establishing a diverse and lucrative retirement portfolio are imperative. I had the opportunity to survey a group of individuals that included members of my family, friends, and some at my church, and asked them why they hesitate to invest but have lofty goals. Here are their top responses:

1. It's not a priority

2. Life issues and emergencies

3. Lack of or stable income source

4. Trust level of financial advisor

5. Assume starting small will have no effect

6. Lack of knowledge

7. Low risk tolerance

Let's change this thought process. Remember, change your habits change your circumstances and wealth. Reasons I shared why they should:

1. Retirement is coming!!! (Don't want to work your entire life)

2. Can't leave free money on the table with employer sponsored 401k

3. Let your money work for you. (Growth based on interest rates)

4. Have to understand time value of money (Earlier you begin the more time you have for your money to grow and less aggressive you have to be due to time constraints if you begin in your latter years) (See example below)

The Story of Two Savers

Saver A spends his money partying for 8 years, then opens a tax-deferred account earning 12% at age 26 and invests $150/Month for the next 40 years

Contributions = $72,000

Saver B invests $150/Month for 8 years in a tax-deferred account earning 12% and saves NOTHING for the next 40 years

Contributions = $14,400

Which saver ends up with more money?

Saver A			Saver B		
Age	Annual Amt	Total	Age	Annual Amt	Total
18	$0	$0	18	$1,800	$1,902
19	0	0	19	1,800	4,046
20	0	0	20	1,800	6,462
21	0	0	21	1,800	9,183
22	0	0	22	1,800	12,250
23	0	0	23	1,800	15,706
24	0	0	24	1,800	19,600
25	0	0	25	1,800	23,989
26	1,800	1,902	26	0	26,868
27	1,800	4,046	27	0	30,092
28	1,800	6,462	28	0	33,703
29	1,800	9,183	29	0	37,747
30	1,800	12,250	30	0	42,277
35	1,800	34,506	35	0	74,506
40	1,800	74,937	40	0	131,305
45	1,800	148,388	45	0	231,405
50	1,800	281,827	50	0	407,815
55	1,800	524,245	55	0	718,709
60	1,800	964,644	60	0	1,266,610
65	1,800	1,764,716	65	0	2,232,200

Saver B has outpaced A by over $467,000!!

DON'T PROCRASTINATE

Don't get me wrong; I am aware that there are some people who literally work until their dying day. I'm sure there are those who love their job so much that the idea of one day not doing it anymore is downright unthinkable. But those people—and I think you would agree—are the exception and not the norm. Most people, especially those who have spent the majority of their lives doing some kind of work, want to stop punching the clock and enjoy their families or favorite pastimes in their latter years. They spend years talking about the day when they no longer have to deal with the difficult boss, the chatty coworkers, or the office politics.

But, if you haven't prepared in your prime years, the closer you get to retirement age, the more the thought of it becomes a burden instead of a blessing. How much you do or don't prepare dictates the level of comfort you'll enjoy at retirement. I ask people all the time, why work your entire lives to have to scale back in your older years? This is the time where you should be able to vacation and live stress-free because you've made great decisions! RETIREMENT (AGE) IS COMING. SO, BE PREPARED!

In the *Wisdom Journal*, they provided the following statistics:

- 56 percent have a net worth less than $25,000

- 95 percent of Baby Boomers don't have enough for retirement

- Over 50 percent of Americans didn't save one red cent last year

- 33 percent of Americans admit to having not saved anything at all for retirement

- 60 percent of them have no idea how much they'll need to retire

- 35 percent of Baby Boomers will depend on Social Security alone

- 66 percent will retire with less than $25,000

- 35 percent will retire with less than $10,000

- Just 2 percent of Americans have an adequate pension plan in place

These numbers are startling. And sad. In reality, you may be a part of one or more of these statistics. But, that can change right now.

When you think of what you'd like to live on in your golden years, don't base that figure on your current bills and debts, it should be the other way around. Let your retirement dictate what your bills can be. Remember the following in this order:

1. 10 percent for tithes and offering

2. 10 percent in savings

3. 10 percent invested in your retirement

As a Christian, I tithe. I give God the first 10 percent of my pay. In the New American Standard Bible (NASB) Malachi 3:10 says, "Bring the whole tithe into the storehouse, so that there may be food in My house, and test Me now in this," says the Lord of hosts, "if I will not open for you the windows of heaven and pour out for you a blessing until it overflows." I believe that if I give Him the first ten, He'll bless the remaining ninety. The fact is, He gives us all our resources anyway, so giving Him back a tenth seems more than reasonable to me.

Sol Hicks, President of Solomon Hicks Financial Services, speaker, career coach, and author, puts it well. He says:

> Investing your money and buying insurance boils down to just two things—what you desire, and what you're worth. In other words, every decision you make concerning them should 1) move you closer to the life of your dreams, and/or 2) work to keep your family financially solvent if, God forbid, something happens to

you or your ability to earn an income on your way to the dream. Invest wisely.

I encourage everyone to consult a financial advisor. If you haven't already done so, irrespective of what your current financial situation is, you should start doing research to find an advisor you feel comfortable with. Remember, this person needs to be a part of your Power of Five. Refer to the criteria I gave a few chapters ago to make the right choice. Don't become the prey of financial professionals looking to get rich quick. If you do happen to select the wrong guy, and he's dishonest with about as much integrity as Bernie Madoff, once he realizes you're clueless, you're his next sucker. It's unfortunate, but some financial advisors sell their clients products based on their commission possibilities without an ounce of concern for their client's actual needs.

Once you establish a relationship and choose a financial advisor, you have to begin aggressively preparing for your retirement or college funding for your children. Remember, every year that goes by is one year wasted and forces you to have to be more aggressive by the year. Time waits on no one.

The longer you wait and the older you are will force you to have to diversify to gain larger returns. A savings account will not allow you to retire by the time you are sixty-seven years old. On www.ssa.gov, full retirement age (also called "normal retirement age") had been sixty-five for many years. However, beginning with people born in 1938 or later, that age gradually increases until it reaches sixty-seven for people born after 1959.

The Social Security Administration shares how it works if your full retirement age is sixty-seven.

- If you start your retirement benefits at age sixty-two, your monthly benefit amount is reduced by about 30 percent. The reduction for starting benefits at age

    o Sixty-three is about 25 percent;

    o Sixty-four is about 20 percent;

    o Sixty-five is about 13.3 percent; and

    o Sixty-six is about 6.7 percent.

- If you start receiving spouse's benefits at age sixty-two, your monthly benefit amount is reduced to about 32.5 percent of the amount your spouse would receive if his or her benefits started at full retirement age. (The reduction is about 67.5 percent.) The reduction for starting benefits as a spouse at age

    o Sixty-three is about 65 percent;

    o Sixty-four is about 62.5 percent;

    o Sixty-five is about 58.3 percent;

    o Sixty-six is about 54.2 percent; and

    o Sixty-seven is 50 percent (the maximum benefit amount).

Unless you have above average income or circumstances, especially when the average savings account is paying less than a quarter of a percent in interest, you must invest and consider diversifying to ensure you can receive a decent return. Look below at the various areas breakdown your investments.

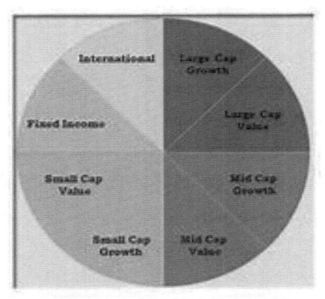

By Diversified Investment Portfolio | Holt-Smith Advisors

Portfolio Diversification:

1. International

2. Large Cap Growth & Value

3. Mid Cap Growth & Value

4. Small Cap Growth & Value

5. Fixed Income

6. Other

Use the formula below to determine your investment diversification model. Use your age to determine what percentage should be invested in conservative products: FDIC insured accounts, CDs, bonds, treasury bills, etc. One hundred minus your current age can be invested large cap, small cap and mid cap investments, international and other areas evenly. To reduce risk in your nest egg, avoid investing in individual companies, and choose mutual funds instead. Keep your industry exposure to a reasonable (even) percentage. See example below.

The information I'm providing you with is meant to assist and educate you on investments. It doesn't eliminate your need to meet with a financial advisor, who is educated, licensed, and likely receiving ongoing training so they can stay current with changes in the market.

Avoid making investment choices on your own and not keeping track of your investment portfolio after that point. When is the last time you looked at your 401k or 403b or even your other investments? If you have, do you understand the statements you receive quarterly? *Exactly!*

Recommended Formula:

If you are twenty-five years old:

One hundred - Your Current Age = Amount Invested in Less Conservative

100-25=75

(By percentages)

Sample 2012 Nest Egg (assuming you are 25)

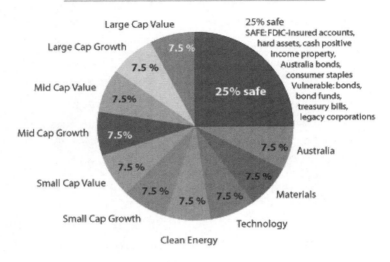

Sample 2012 Nest Egg (assuming you are 50)

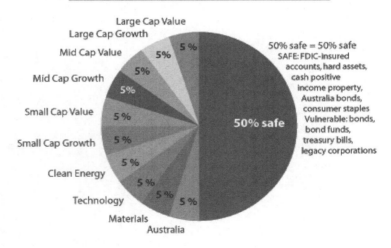

Pie Charts (c) NataliePace.com 2012. Used by permission

Definitions provided by Webster's Dictionary and Investopdia:

IRAs (Investment Retirement Account)

i. **Mutual Funds** -   Open-end investment company that invests money of its shareholders in a usually diversified group of securities of other corporations

ii. **Roth IRA** - Individual Retirement Account that allows contributors to make annual contributions and to withdraw the principal and earnings tax-free under certain conditions. Maximum annual contributions continue to adjust. Allow your advisor to let you know your limits. If you make too much for the Roth, fund a nondeductible IRA and convert it.

iii. **Traditional IRA** - A Traditional IRA is an individual retirement account (IRA) in the United States. The IRA is held at a custodian institution such as a bank or brokerage, and may be invested in anything that the custodian allows. However, the best provision of a Traditional IRA — the tax-deductibility of contributions — has strict eligibility requirements based on income, filing status, and availability of other retirement plans. Transactions in the account, including interest, dividends, and capital gains, are not subject to tax while still in the account, but upon withdrawal from the account, withdrawals are subject to federal income tax.

Roth vs. Traditional

Unlike the Roth IRA, the only criterion for being eligible to contribute to a Traditional IRA is sufficient income to make the contribution. This is in contrast to a Roth IRA, in which contributions are never tax-deductible, but qualified withdrawals are tax-free. The traditional IRA also has more restrictions on withdrawals than a Roth IRA. With both types of IRA, transactions inside the account (including capital gains, dividends, and interest) incur no tax liability.

iv. **401k** - A retirement savings plan that is funded by employee contributions and (often) matching contributions from the employer; contributions are made from your salary before taxes and the funds grow tax-free until they are withdrawn, at which point they can be converted into an IRA; funds can be transferred if you change employers and you can (to some extent) manage the investments yourself.

v. **403b** - A retirement plan for certain employees of public schools, tax-exempt organizations and certain ministers. Generally, retirement income accounts can invest in either annuities or mutual funds. Also known as a "tax-sheltered annuity (TSA) plan."

vi. **SEP (Simplified Employee Pension) -** A retirement plan that an employer or self-employed individuals can establish. The employer is allowed a tax deduction for contributions made to the SEP plan and makes contributions to each eligible employee's SEP IRA on a discretionary basis. Immediately 100 percent vested.

vii. **Annuity**- an insurance policy or an investment that pays someone a fixed amount of money each year. Sold by financial institutions that is designed to accept and grow funds from an individual and then, upon annuitization, pay out a stream of payments to the individual at a later point in time. Annuities are primarily used as a means of securing a steady cash flow for an individual during their retirement years.

viii. **Stocks** - Buy stocks like socks...good quality and on sale. Ownership of a corporation indicated by shares, which represent a piece of the corporation's assets and earnings.

ix. **Bonds** - Bonds are debt and are issued for a period of more than one year. The US government, local governments, water districts, companies and many other types of institutions sell bonds. When an investor buys bonds, he or she is lending money. The seller of the bond agrees to repay the principal amount of the loan at a specified time. Interest-bearing bonds pay interest periodically.

x. **IDA** (Investment Development Account) - This is an account that will match you for every $1 you save you will receive a $2 match. These funds are normally to assist families with education, home buying and for starting a new business. Economic and Community Development Institute (ECDI) defines Individual Development Accounts (IDAs) as matched savings accounts that enable families to save, build assets, and enter the financial mainstream. IDAs reward the monthly savings of income eligible families who are building towards purchasing an asset - most commonly buying their first home, paying for post-secondary education, or starting a small business (www.cfed.org). Visit www.ecdi.org to gather further details and to determine if you meet the income guidelines.

The chart below displays a rate of return for a period of forty years. It assumes an initial contribution of $2,000 and a $2,000 contribution made every year with all dividends, capital gains, distributions, and interest reinvested and no distributions. It displays a forty year period of time with various interest rates.

The earlier you invest the better off you will be because you have more years to save and more time for your money to earn interest and grow. Also, you don't want the pressure of having only ten years left to save for the rest of your life by waiting too late to start. You have no time to lose; figure out what your options are and begin to invest today.

Annual Rate of Return						
YEARS	6%	8%	10%	12%	15%	20%
0	$2,000	$2,000	$2,000	$2,000	$2,000	$2,000
1	$4,120	$4,160	$4,200	$4,240	$4,300	$4,400
2	$6,367	$6,493	$6,620	$6,749	$6,945	$7,280
3	$8,749	$9,012	$9,282	$9,559	$9,987	$10,736
4	$11,274	$11,733	$12,210	$12,706	$13,485	$14,883
5	$13,951	$14,672	$15,431	$16,230	$17,507	$19,860
6	$16,788	$17,846	$18,974	$20,178	$22,134	$25,832
7	$19,795	$21,273	$22,872	$24,599	$27,454	$32,998
8	$22,983	$24,975	$27,159	$29,551	$33,572	$41,598
9	$26,362	$28,973	$31,875	$35,097	$40,607	$51,917

10	$29,943	$33,291	$37,062	$41,309	$48,699	$64,301
11	$33,740	$37,954	$42,769	$48,266	$58,003	$79,161
12	$37,764	$42,991	$49,045	$56,058	$68,704	$96,993
13	$42,030	$48,430	$55,950	$64,785	$81,009	$118,392
14	$46,552	$54,304	$63,545	$74,559	$95,161	$144,070
15	$51,345	$60,649	$71,899	$85,507	$111,435	$174,884
16	$56,426	$67,500	$81,089	$97,767	$130,150	$211,861
17	$61,811	$47,900	$91,198	$111,499	$151,673	$256,233
18	$67,520	$82,893	$102,318	$126,879	$176,424	$309,480
19	$73,571	$91,524	$114,550	$144,105	$204,887	$373,376
20	$79,985	$100,846	$128,005	$163,397	$237,620	$450,051
25	$118,313	$159,909	$218,364	$300,668	$491,424	$1,134,755
30	$169,603	$246,642	$363,887	$542,585	$1,001,914	$2,838,516
35	$238,242	$374,204	$598,254	$968,926	$2,028,691	$7,078,019
40	$330,095	$561,562	$975,704	$1,720,285	$4,093,908	$17,627,259

WISE CHOICES: *Invest in Your Future*

Investment Tips (Forbes 2014 Investment Guide)

- Build an emergency fund of at least $1000.00. Use the 52 Week Money challenge. Don't undervalue the importance of liquidity. Having cash readily available will be important for emergencies.

- Participate in your job's 401k or 403b retirement options to receive employer match for your contributions. Don't leave free money on the table. When you get a raise, use at least a portion of your increase to add to the amount you invest every month.

- Make changes to your investment allocations yearly. Pay attention to your investment; it's your money and your responsibility. Diversify but don't overdo it.

- Fund a Roth IRA. Funds grow tax-free and in certain emergency circumstances you can take contribution back without penalty.

- Make sure you update your beneficiaries annually to verify life changes, divorce, or death of a family member, etc.

- Raise the deductibles on your auto, renters, and home insurance to reduce monthly premium costs.

- Beat death taxes in some states by making big gifts while you're alive.

- For a simple tax-free wealth transfer, make $14,000 in annual gifts to children and grandchildren. It won't cut into your $5.25 million lifetime exemption from gift and estate taxes.

- Add a personal items floater to your homeowner's insurance to cover collectibles, jewelry and other expensive items.

- Keep your eye on mutual fund fees and expenses.

- Recommended systems to use: QuickBooks Online, Quicken, Mint.com to track finances.

- Find a local charity to work for to get a portion of your federal student debt reduced after ten years.

- Don't accept high property tax assessments. Dispute them with your county auditor's office. Go to your county auditor's website and search for real estate tax reassessment or valuation. Contact the office and discuss deadlines to turn in assessment forms.

College Payment Options

"The Top Fifteen Personal Finance Statistics That Will Blow Your Mind" by Hank Coleman states that students graduate with an average of $23,186 in student loan debt and $4,100 credit card debt. Make sure you are saving for your child's college education to prevent them from having to acquire debt. If they are going to college immediately, consider making withdrawals from your IRAs (not your 401k) to pay their tuition. Before tackling the college expense on your own do some research it is still a high possibility that your child can find resources to either bridge the gap of the difference or to pay their entire college expenses. Also utilize their high school counselor for advice about resources or direction.

Use the following websites to assist with college funding, resources, and counseling.

www.collegeadvantage.com

www.collegenowgc.org

www.savingsforcollege.com

www.fafsa.ed.gov

Now let's discuss what the next steps are with getting funding for college.

FAFSA (Free Application for Federal Student Aid)

Info gathered at www.fafsa.ed.gov describes Free Application for Federal Student Aid as a part of the U.S. Department of Education. It is the largest provider of student financial aid in the nation. FAFSA provides more than $150 billion in federal grants, loans, and work-study funds each year to more than fifteen million students paying for college or career school.

FAFSA is responsible for managing the student financial assistance programs authorized under Title IV of the Higher Education Act of 1965. These programs provide grants, loans, and work-study funds to students attending college or career school.   FAFSA ensures students and their families can benefit from these programs.

The duties of www.fafsa.ed.gov is listed below:

- Informs students and families about the availability of the federal student aid programs and the process for applying for and receiving aid from those programs

- Responsible for developing the *Free Application for Federal Student Aid* (*FAFSA*SM)

- Responsible for disbursing, reconciling, and accounting for all federal student aid funds that are delivered to students each year

- Responsible for managing the outstanding *federal student loan* portfolio and securing repayment from federal student loan borrowers

- Offers free assistance to students, parents, and borrowers throughout the entire financial aid process

What You Need to Know About the Free Application for Federal Student Aid (FAFSA)

- Online application that is filled out annually using parents' and students' tax records from the prior year

- Once reviewed, a student may be given a certain amount in awards

- Award amount will be comprised of both loans and grants, depending upon income and need

- The FAFSA needs to be filled out each year, and the awards offered last from fall of the year the application is completed through the end of the following summer semester

Student Loans

CNNMoney.com states that one of the most common types of financing options is student loans. These accrue interest over time and usually require payments to be made on them starting about six months after a student leaves school. There are two main types of student loans: government and private loans.

1. Subsidized Federal Loans

2. Unsubsidized Federal Loans

3. Federal Plus Loans

4. Federal Perkins Loans

5. Private Lenders

Federal loans are preferable primarily because they have an interest rate with a fixed cap set by Congress. They come as either as unsubsidized loans, which accrue interest while the student is still in school, or as subsidized loans, where the government pays the interest until after a student graduates or leaves college.

One popular federal loan is the Stafford loan. Private loans have, for the most part, higher interest rates than federal loans. These rates can also fluctuate over time and also can be determined by credit score and other factors. Remember most financial institutions offer students loans, so discuss options with your banker. Ask about 529 Plans or Coverdell Savings Plans.

529 College Savings Plan

Visit www.collegeadvantage.com to retrieve further info about 529 College Savings Plan. Investopedia defines a 529 plan as a plan that allows for the prepayment of qualified higher education expenses at eligible educational institutions, also known as a "qualified tuition program" or fully known as a section 529 plan.

The prepayment may be in the form of a contribution to an account established specifically for paying higher educational expenses. There is no income restriction for individuals who want to contribute to a 529 plan; however, because contributions cannot exceed the amount that sufficiently covers the expenses of the beneficiary's qualified higher education, individuals should take care not to over-fund the 529 plan.

Coverdell Education Savings Account (ESA)

An account created as an incentive to help parents and students save for education expenses. Visit www.irs.gov to retrieve further info about this option. Investorwords.com defines an ESA as an investment vehicle designed to help parents fund their child's education. The Coverdell Education Savings Account has replaced the Education IRA. Contributions to the account are taxed, but earnings used to pay education expenses are not. The account is transferable among family members. However, there are several restrictions attached to this account. The entire account has to be disbursed before the beneficiary's thirtieth birthday, and any withdrawals after this date or for expenses that do not qualify under the act will be subject to income taxes and a penalty.

Grants

Grants are another way to finance college tuition expenses. The advantage of grants is that students don't have to pay them back. The most popular grant is the federal Pell Grant. This is awarded to students who demonstrate financial need by completing the FAFSA. The Pell Grant offers students differing amounts depending on their need. This amount differs annually. The case is the same for most other grants as well.

Scholarships

Scholarships are another important means of college financing for many students. Almost every institution offers a number of scholarships, each one with different criteria for those who are eligible to receive them. Often they require a certain GPA. Scholarships may also require an essay, community service project, majoring in a specific field of study or artistic piece to receive them. Scholarship money is not a loan and therefore does not need to be paid back. There are also many private scholarships not associated with colleges and universities.

Locate local organizations and foundations that have scholarship dollars available based on certain criteria. For example, Northeastern Ohio residents visit www.clevelandfoundation.org to see what scholarships are available.

Understanding Default

Like medical bills students leave college and disregard student loans. These loans cannot be eliminated by the filing of bankruptcy. NEVER ignore delinquency or default notices from your loan servicer. If you don't make your monthly loan payments, you will become delinquent on your student loan and risk going into default. You want to avoid default it will ruin your credit, affecting job opportunities and possibly the purchase of your new home.

Contact the loan provider if you are finding it difficult to make timely payments. There are options. Since this is such an issue with both college dropouts and graduates I want to discuss how to avoid or get out of default.

On FAFSA's website, they share the following information:

If in default, any William D. Ford Federal Direct Loan (Direct Loan) Program loan or Federal Family Education Loan (FFEL) Program loan that is owned by the U.S. Department of Education (ED) is assigned to ED's Default Resolution Group for collection. Defaulted

FFEL Program loans that are not owned by ED will be assigned to a guaranty agency for collection. For defaulted Federal Perkins Loans, you'll need to check with the school from which you borrowed to find out about loan repayment.

If you are unsure which type(s) of loan(s) you have, check your original loan documents or use the National Student Loan Data System (NSLDS®). *Will only display federal loans.

You have three options for getting your loan out of default: repayment, rehabilitation, or consolidation

Loan Repayment

One option for getting out of default is repaying your defaulted student loan in full. Get repayment information at www.fafsa.ed.gov for your loan(s) to learn about how to repay and where to send payments.

Loan Rehabilitation

The second option to rehabilitate your Direct Loan or FFEL Program loan, you and ED must agree on a reasonable and affordable payment plan. (Remember, contact your school for your Perkins Loan). Your loan is rehabilitated only after you have voluntarily made the agreed-upon payments on time and the loan has been purchased by a lender.

Once your loan is rehabilitated, you may regain eligibility for benefits that were available on your loan before you defaulted. Those benefits may include deferment, forbearance, a choice of repayment plans, loan forgiveness, and eligibility for additional federal student aid.

Other benefits of loan rehabilitation include the removal of

- the default status on your defaulted loan

- the default status reported to the national credit bureaus

- wage garnishment, and any withholding of your income tax refund made by the Internal Revenue Service (IRS)

Late payments reported before the loan defaulted will not be removed from your credit report.

Loan Consolidation

Final option for getting out of default is through loan consolidation. Loan consolidation allows you to pay off the outstanding combined balance(s) for one or more federal student loans to create a new single loan with a fixed *interest rate*.

A defaulted *federal student loan* may be included in a consolidation loan after you've made arrangements with ED and made several voluntary payments (contact your school for information about making payments on a Perkins Loan).

Consolidate your loan(s) through a Direct Consolidation Loan. Visit www.loanconsolidation.ed.gov for further details.

Once in default you must make timely agreed upon payments for:

- Three months to consolidate loans

- Six months to be eligible for additional federal aid

- Nine months for loans to be back in good status on credit report; removal of default

College Resources

Any items you may have questions about, contact:

FAFSA

www.fafsa.ed.gov

1-800-4FED-AID

College NOW

www.collegenow.org

Saving for College

www.savingsforcollege.com

1-(585) 286-5426

Upromise

www.upromise.com

1-800-UPROMISE

Student Loan Glossary

Default

Failure to repay a loan according to the terms agreed to in the promissory note. For most federal student loans, you will default if you have not made a payment in more than 270 days.

Direct Loan

A federal student loan, made through the William D. Ford Federal Direct Loan Program, for which eligible students and parents borrow directly from the U.S. Department of Education at participating.

Federal Family Education Loan (FFEL) Program

Under this program, private lenders provide loans to students that are guaranteed by the federal government. These loans include Subsidized Federal Stafford Loans, Unsubsidized Federal Stafford.

FFEL Program

Federal Family Education Loan Program

Guaranty Agency

A state agency or a private, nonprofit organization that administers Federal Family Education Loan (FFEL) Program loans.

Lender

The organization that made the loan initially; the lender could be the borrower's school; a bank, credit union, or other lending institution; or the U.S. Department of Education.

Collection Costs

Expenses charged on defaulted federal student loans that are added to the outstanding principal balance of the loan. These expenses can be up to 18.5 percent of the principal and interest.

Principal

The total sum of money borrowed plus any interest that has been capitalized.

Deferment

A postponement of payment on a loan that is allowed under certain conditions and during which interest does not accrue on Direct Subsidized Loans, Subsidized Federal Stafford Loans, and Federal Perkins Loan.

Forbearance

A period during which your monthly loan payments are temporarily suspended or reduced; your lender may grant you forbearance if you are willing but unable to make loan payments, due to certain financial hardships.

Loan Forgiveness

The cancellation of all or some portion of your remaining federal student loan balance; if your loan is forgiven, you are no longer responsible for repaying that remaining portion of the loan.

Federal Student Aid

Financial aid from the federal government to help you pay for education expenses at an eligible college or career school. Grants, loans and work-study are types of federal student aid.

Interest Rate

The percentage at which interest is calculated on your loan(s)

Federal Student Loan

A loan funded by the federal government to help pay for your education. A federal student loan is borrowed money you must repay with interest.

Direct Consolidation Loan

A federal loan made by the U.S. Department of Education that allows you to combine one or more federal student loans into one new loan. As a result of consolidation, you will only have to make one monthly payment versus multiple payments.

10

WHO'S IN THE WILL?

Necessary Legal Documents

Every prudent man acts with knowledge, but a fool displays folly. (Proverbs 13:16 NASB)

Most people don't consider creating living wills or wills, trusts, and power-of-attorney documents. What I would like for you to avoid is allowing your loved ones' estate to get tied up in the court system. It can become time consuming and expensive with court and legal fees, and possible travel and lodging fees.

The last thing you want to happen if an unexpected tragedy occurs is to send your family into an uproar from lack of preparation or discussion about your important wishes. Your family members will have varying opinions on how your assets and belongings should be divided and how things should be taken care of in general. Eliminate this unnecessary drama by having your paperwork in order well before you (or your family) actually need it. If you don't, you're essentially passing that responsibility on to others who may not be equipped to make those kinds of decisions, especially when they're grieving. Even worse, disagreements about how to handle your estate can cause your family to split. You better believe there will be differing opinions about whether you wanted to be resuscitated or not, cremated or buried, and any other possible point of contention. These questions will arise, and they will be much easier to answer if there is a guide outlining your wishes.

Later in the chapter, I'll list documents that you need to sit with your immediate family members and create if you haven't already done so. (This is another reason why I mentioned having an attorney in your Power of Five. Their expertise can be vital as you try to navigate your way through this process). As you draft these documents, it's important that you are not the only person privy to the information or it defeats the purpose. Place the documents in a safe, secure place. You may want to even consider purchasing an affordable water and fire resistant safe or renting a safe deposit box at your local bank. Whatever you do, make the proper family members aware of where all of these documents are organized. When something unforeseen happens, you will not be able to give instructions. I would also advise you to give access to at least one trustworthy individual outside of your immediate family. If you have children of adult age, consider giving them copies of these documents. Once these documents are completed or prepared, call a family meeting to discuss. Your death isn't the most exciting thing to talk about, but it is important.

I work at "THE WORD" Church and we bury people every year. Most families are unprepared for the loss of their loved one. In most cases, there is no insurance, no will, nor are there any post-death instructions. Many of the disagreements stem from where the funeral should be held due to the differences in church homes and funeral layout. Visit the following sites to create or retrieve further info about these documents. Remember, this is where the relationship with a family attorney is necessary; let people do what they do. Educate yourself so you are prepared and know what to look for. Attorneys charge by the hour or by retainer, but the clock is always ticking. Lawinfo.com assists with finding an attorney in your area. The websites below can help you with forms and legal jargon.

1. www.Legalzoom.com

2. www.Findlaw.com

3. www.Lawdepot.com

The above websites can assist with the areas listed below:

1. Will & Power of Attorney

2. Corporate Forms

3. Rent and Lease Forms

4. Real Estate Forms

5. Sales Related Forms

6. Eviction or Lease

7. Loan or Debt

My attorney, Mitchell Yelsky of Cleveland, Ohio, makes the following statements when it comes to finances:

> We all need money. No one can live without it. The trick is living within your means to achieve financial freedom. This is not easy to do, especially in the consumer society in which we live. We all have to change the way our minds have been programmed by the retailers and advertisers, that if we do not have the latest gadgets or smartphones our lives will not be fulfilled. Our lives are more fulfilled by paying our rent or mortgage on time, by not overextending ourselves with easily available credit that we can't afford to repay and by living within our financial means.

> If you can achieve financial freedom, while you may not be driving the newest or fanciest car, or while you may not be using the newest "must have" smartphone, you will have financial independence. IF you can change the way our consumer minds think, and prioritize the payment of your rent or mortgage over

obtaining the latest fashion or gadget, your life will actually improve.

Overextending yourself financially, to have the latest gadget, or to drive a fancier car, will not result in greater fulfillment. When we can't pay our rent or mortgage, when we can't pay our credit card debt, when we can't meet our financial obligations, we are sued by collection companies and brought into court. Once this happens, it has a negative effect on the way we feel about ourselves, and things begin to spiral out of control financially. It is like a house of cards falling down. One collection leads to another collection and before you know it, you will be consulting with a bankruptcy lawyer.

For most Americans, the most valuable asset that we own is our home. We all work hard to buy a home, and we all put a lot of pride in our homes. Most Americans' single most valuable asset is their house. Upon our death, we want the wealth that we've accumulated, to pass on to our loved ones, so estate planning is as important a part of achieving financial freedom, as is paying our debt and bills on time.

The type of estate planning you need is a function of the wealth that you have accumulated. A factory worker in Pittsburgh, who paid his mortgage off in full after thirty years of working in that factory has different estate planning needs than a wealthy businessperson. Families who have special needs children have different estate planning needs than a family with no children.

Because we've worked so hard to achieve financial freedom, we should also be equally as mindful that the wealth we have accumulated during our lives should be passed on to our loved ones, not to our bill collectors. Most lawyers that do estate planning typically provide a free initial consultation, so the only thing you have to lose by speaking with an estate planning lawyer to gather facts and information, is a little bit of your time. It is strongly recommended to have a comprehensive state plan in place, so that the financial freedom you achieved during your life can be passed on to your loved ones after your death.

The documents below don't substitute the need for legal advice, and this list is not meant to be comprehensive; but, this will give you a great starting point.

Legal Document Websites

www.legalzoom.com

www.Estate.findlaw.com

www.freelegaldocument.com

Another option: Purchase Quicken Will Maker Plus

(www.Amazon.com)

List of Suggested Documents:

Below is a list of some important documents that will assist you and your family in dealing with difficult situations if a family member becomes incapacitated or dies. Make sure when creating these documents you conduct an annual review to ensure you haven't decided to change beneficiaries or add an additional beneficiary.

Webster's dictionary defines a beneficiary as a person that receives assets or profits from an estate, trust, an insurance policy or any instrument in which there is distribution. I have witnessed husbands divorce their wives and forget to change them as the beneficiary on a life insurance policy and the ex-wife receives the entire benefit upon their death, due to the insured forgetting to make a change of beneficiary to his current wife. At that point the new wife has to take the ex-wife to court and try to prove that she was entitled to the benefit. The simplest place to ensure you have a beneficiary and continue to update is your bank accounts. It literally takes minutes to have your bank handle this matter.

1. Health Insurance Portability and Accountability Act (HIPAA) Release:

HIPAA is the "Health Insurance Portability and Accountability Act." It dictates how health information is distributed. To give someone access to your records you must sign off on this document. Every doctor and every hospital has HIPAA release documents you can sign that gives them permission to share information with the person designated.

2. Power of Attorney (POA) for Health Care:

If you are too ill to make decisions, you must give someone the authority to make decisions your behalf authority. The POA for Health Care is the document that specifies who this person is, and what limits, if any, you have placed on their decision-making authority. Most hospitals will provide these documents but I recommend that you prepare them before you need them.

3. **Living Will:** The living will is the document that specifies what kind of treatment you do or do not want if you are extremely ill with no hope of recovery. Most hospitals will provide these documents but I recommend that you prepare them before you need them.

4. **Durable Power of Attorney (DPOA):**

The definition provided by www.pbs.org for DPOA is a document that grants a person or persons ("Attorney-in-fact") you trust, the legal powers to perform on your behalf, certain acts and functions specifically outlined in the document. This power is effective immediately and continues even if the grantor becomes disabled or incompetent. The powers usually granted include real estate, banking and financial transactions, personal and family maintenance, government benefits, estate trust, and beneficiary transactions. Because it can involve complex financial decisions the Durable Power of Attorney should be drawn up by a lawyer.

5. **Last Will and Testament:**

It is important to have a will, which distributes your possessions after you are gone. We never think when we depart our family that it is our final goodbye, but final goodbyes are inevitable. If you should die without a will, the court will decide who gets what. Based on the complexity of your estate, this document should also be written by a lawyer, who will make sure your instructions are addressed and implemented and that your will meets state laws. In most cases, you could be looking at just a few hundred dollars to have this document created.

6. **Do Not Resuscitate Order (DNR):**

This document states that you do not want actions such as CPR or intubation in the event your heart or breathing stops. This document should be kept in an easily visible location where those who know to honor your wishes can locate. This is always a hard decision for families as family members have varying opinions.

7. **Kids Protection Plan**

For parents with young children. The Kids Protection Plan is a set of documents that ensures that your kids are taken care of, not just in the long term, but in the short term as well. In the documents you can name guardianship for the long term for the people you want to raise your kids and make their health care and education decisions. But for the short term, the Kids Protection Plan also allows you to dictate what should be done with your kids in full details, even broken down to what happens in every year of their lives until they become adults, following death or incapacitation.

8. **Financial Love Letter**

I was given this idea from Sol Hicks, internationally sought-after speaker, career coach, and consultant based in Atlanta, Georgia. Purchase a binder to organize and keep all the documents listed in this chapter. It should also include the following other documents:

- A copy of all your bank and investments accounts

- A list of all current credit cards or loans and any all other debts

- A list of all insurance policies, mortgage, renters, and life insurance

- A copy of driver's licenses, birth certificates, and social security cards of all immediate family members

9. Trust (In Addition To a Will)

Most people think estate planning or having your affairs in order means having a will, but that's a misconception. The will only tells the court what to do with your assets, but it doesn't keep your family out of court. In fact, the will can put them in court for completely public and expensive proceedings. A trust, instead, is often a better option.

The trust is what keeps the family out of court and will make things as easy as possible for your loved ones. It spells out exactly what you want to happen to your assets and who you want to take care of things for you.

Individuals may control the distribution of their property during their lives or after their deaths through the use of a trust. There are many types of trusts and many purposes for their creation. A trust may be created for the financial benefit of the person creating the trust, a surviving spouse or minor children, or a charitable purpose. Though a variety of trusts are permitted by law, trust arrangements that are attempts to evade creditors or lawful responsibilities will be declared void by the courts.

The law of trusts is voluminous and often complicated, but generally it is concerned with whether a trust has been created, whether it is a public or private trust, whether it is legal, and whether the trustee has lawfully managed the trust and trust property. The most obvious way to avoid probate is to make sure that the property isn't yours when you die. Most people accomplish this by giving away property as gifts during their life. Be aware, however, that gift taxes apply if the gift is in excess of a certain amount, so this is typically a good option only if the asset is below the gift tax threshold. Some assets, like money, can be split into smaller payments and paid over a series of years to avoid the gift tax.

Most people have probably heard that it's a good idea to avoid probate, though they may not fully understand why. Essentially, the reason you may wish to avoid probate is because it's extremely time consuming and expensive, often tying up property for months, and almost always requiring the assistance of an attorney. The best way to avoid probate, therefore, is to simply line up your assets so that there is nothing in your name that does not automatically pass to someone else at your death. To learn more about avoiding probate, choose from the list of titles below.

10. Estate Plan

It's not just the rich who need estate plans. Estate planning is a matter of figuring out how to structure and arrange your assets so that you pass on as much as possible to your heirs, on your own terms. If you don't have one in place, let this chapter be motivation to get your plan completed. Doing so will save time, money, and possibly grief.

Visit www.irs.gov. It will share information about how to handle taxes that deal with an estate.

Estates may also have to pay tax on the total value of assets if the estate is valued at more than $5,250,000. The estate tax is a tax on assets, whereas the estate income tax is a tax on income. For more information or further details about estates taxes consult your estate attorney or CPA, and also visit www.irs.gov.

The probate process is like a will; something you hear you need to have or at least understand. The most common question you hear when it comes to probate is, "What can I do to avoid the costly attorney and court fees, possibly up to 5 percent of the entire estate value and the lengthy process that could take months and even more than a year to complete?" Some of the costs could include executor, attorney, and court (to include appraisers) fees.

Probate

Probate is a court-supervised process of distributing and overseeing property after a person dies. The purpose of probate is to determine the wishes of the deceased, pay debts, and to distribute the property according to the decedent's wishes. The following occurs during probate:

- Determination of the executor or the appointment of an administrator

- Authentication of the will

- Identification and inventory of the decedent's property

- Identification of heirs and beneficiaries

- Payment of debts and taxes

- Distribution of property according to a will or according to state law

Many individuals take into consideration avoiding probate in deciding on an estate planning option.

Common questions:

1. **Is avoiding probate possible through probate exemptions?**

Yes, in some states the law provides a way of avoiding probate by allowing an exemption or a simplified probate process for small estates only worth a certain amount. In California, for example, small estates worth less than $100,000 escape the probate process. In a few states, probate is eliminated or a simplified probate process applies for property left to the surviving spouse.

2. **If avoiding probate is not an option, who is responsible for managing the probate process?**

An executor named in a will or an administrator appointed by a probate court is responsible for overseeing the probate process. A probate judge appoints an administrator if an executor is unnamed in a will or if the decedent died without a will. Usually, the administrator is a relative or the person inheriting the majority of the decedent's estate.

The executor or the administrator performs the following duties:

- Obtains the decedents original will

- If necessary, hires a probate attorney

- Initiates and manages the probate process

- Cancels credit cards

- Notifies government entities of the decedents death

- Manages assets

In many situations, the executor oversees probate, while a probate lawyer performs the bulk of the work.

If probate proceedings are unnecessary, the family of the decedent chooses an informal estate representative to pay debts and to distribute the property. Usually the estate representative is a family member or a close friend of the decedent.

3. What happens during the probate process?

Because probate involves court costs and attorney fees, avoiding probate will save time and money. The probate process usually takes between six months to a year. The executor of the will or a court-appointed administrator will handle probate, and, if necessary, hire a probate attorney. The executor or the administrator is responsible for filing the appropriate paperwork with the probate court after the decedent's death.

During probate, the following occurs: the probate court receives a copy of the decedents will, probate assets are identified and inventoried, contact is made with heirs, beneficiaries, and creditors, and debts and taxes are paid. The last step in the probate process is the distribution of probate assets. In some situations, the executor may have to sell assets, such as real estate and securities, to pay outstanding debts or to make cash bequests specified by the will.

4. What are my options for avoiding probate?

If property qualifies for a state's exemption or a simplified probate process, probate is inapplicable and it is unnecessary to devise methods to avoid probate. If, on the other hand, an estate will be subject to probate, there are some effective methods of avoiding probate.

Naming a Beneficiary: The owner of an account can designate a person to inherit it upon their death. While the owner retains control while alive, the property transfers to the named beneficiary upon the owner's death. In many states, naming a beneficiary is available for pay-on-death bank accounts, transfer-on-death securities, and in a few states, it is possible to create transfer-on-death deeds for real estate and transfer-on-death vehicle registration.

Jointly Owned Property: By jointly owning property with someone, when you die the ownership of the property can simply transfer to that person rather than pass through probate. There are several forms of jointly-owned property. Here are the most common:

- **Joint Tenancy with a Right of Survivorship** - As the name suggests, you take property as "joint tenants" and upon the death of a joint tenant, the surviving tenant takes the deceased tenant's portion.

- **Tenancy by the Entirety** - This is a form of ownership only available to married couples (and some same-sex couples in a few states). It works in much the same way as a joint tenancy with a right of survivorship, in that effectively upon the death of one spouse, the living spouse takes the deceased spouse's portion.

- **Community Property** - In community property states, married couples can hold property as community property with the right of survivorship. It has the same effect upon the death of one spouse as a tenancy by the entirety, where the surviving spouse takes full ownership of the property.

- **Revocable Living Trusts** - Living trusts avoid probate because you effectively grant the trustee (the person overseeing the trust) the ownership of property. Thus, when you die it is the trustee transferring property, not you. You can instruct the trustee that, upon your death, he or she should transfer the property held in trust to your family and friends. This effectively transfers property but lets you sidestep probate court. Trusts are set up in formal documents, much like a will, so make sure that you comply with your state's requirements for a trust when setting one up.

Payable on Death (POD) Accounts - Like their name suggests, POD accounts are simply accounts with an instruction that, upon your death, the account transfers to a beneficiary that you name. They are extremely simple to set up, with most banks simply requiring that you fill out a form naming the beneficiary. POD accounts are popular because, in addition to being simple to setup, you can spend the money as you see fit during your lifetime and the beneficiary has no right to the money. Similarly, it is extremely easy for a beneficiary to collect on a POD. The beneficiary simply shows up to the bank with the proper identification and collects the account.

Retirement Accounts - An increasingly popular option to avoid probate is the use of retirement accounts, specifically IRA and 401k accounts. When you establish these accounts, you will be asked to name a beneficiary of the account upon your death. As a single person, you are free to name whomever you want, but be aware that as a married person, your spouse may inherently have a right to some or all of the money in a retirement account.

Transfer on Death Registrations - Many states allow you to transfer securities (stocks, bonds, brokerage accounts) as well as vehicles and still avoid probate. Much like POD accounts, you will sign a registration statement that declares who you want your securities or vehicles to pass to upon your death.

Gifts -The most obvious way to avoid probate is to make sure that the property isn't yours when you die. Most people accomplish this by giving away property as gifts during their life. Be aware, however, that gift taxes apply if the gift is in excess of a certain amount, so this is typically a good option only if the asset is below the gift tax threshold. Some assets, like money, can be split into smaller payments and paid over a series of years to avoid the gift tax.

Most people have probably heard that it's a good idea to avoid probate, though they may not fully understand why. Essentially, the reason you may wish to avoid probate is because it's extremely time consuming and expensive, often tying up property for months, and almost always requiring the assistance of an attorney. The best way to avoid probate, therefore, is to simply line up your assets so that there is nothing in your name that does not automatically pass to someone else at your death.

While these items may not seem important at this point, they will be vital if you become extremely ill or go to Heaven unexpectedly; so save your family the headache and heartache. Two dates that are guaranteed are your birthdate and your death date. Prepare for the latter and challenge those around you to get these documents prepared and properly filed.

Sol Hicks says it well, "When you know what really matters to you, you can put financial income, assets, and resources in their proper place—as a servant and not your master. Then you will have taken the first steps toward long-term financial security. Protect what you have worked for and your family."

11

YOUNG MONEY

Youth and Their Finances

A good man leaves an inheritance to his children's children, and the wealth of the sinner is stored up for the righteous. (Proverbs 13:22 NASB)

Parenting is difficult. There are many lessons to teach our kids and only a few years to inculcate the really important stuff before the media, friends, and other outside influences take hold and flood their impressionable consciousness with things that at best, we'd rather not have them exposed to, and at worst, we have to go back and try to fix later. To that end, it's important that number one, from the time they are born, we live right in front of them. Number two, we teach them our values; and number three, we give them access to the right information (the Word of God and other edifying books, church programs that teach responsibility and accountability, educational podcasts, etc.) and encourage them to use it as soon as they are able to communicate.

Whether you're proud to admit it or not, you can probably think of a habit or two that came straight from your lineage. How many times do you hear people say to daughters after hearing the way they speak to younger siblings, "You sound just like your mother," or to sons after witnessing how they handle conflict, "You act just like your father"? Some of our habits and behaviors are simply imbedded in us, through no mindful integration of our own. We mimic and live what we've observed from those around us for years, and you know this: it's often what we've seen—not what we've heard—that we grow up and repeat.

This isn't a parenting book, but I've got some advice for those of you with children. (Consider it a bonus). When it comes to money and money management, lead by example. It's not enough to simply tell your children what to do and what not to do. They need to be included in (certain) conversations about money and taught through observation the proper and improper ways of handling their finances.

When you're doing the budget, take some time to explain to your children why it's important to have a financial plan. Tell them about your real life experiences to help them avoid making the same mistakes. While you may not be comfortable with disclosing how much you make with your children, be candid when talking about the significance of earning a living, setting a budget, saving, and spending. Even in times of financial strain, be open. I am not saying to tell your ten year old that they're going to have to help make the rent or mortgage payment because you're broke; however, you can find creative ways to inform your children of when things are a little tighter than normal, and express what you could, should, or will do differently to make sure everyone in the house is taken care of.

Kids are intuitive, so if you're like millions of Americans who experience financial hardship every year, your kids will be able to pick up on the fact that something is different in the house. They may sense the stress or tension. Protect them by letting them know that you will not allow them to go hungry or be outdoors, but respect them by being honest and telling them they may not be dining out for a while, and they may have to sacrifice some extras. If you establish a good rapport with your children early, they'll take these conversations in stride, feeling like they are a part of the solution. As they get older, this will speak volumes to their sense of self-worth and confidence, another invaluable consequence of your honesty.

The biggest mistake you can make is assuming that your children will know how to handle money because you've had superficial conversations with them. ("You're not going to the movies because we don't have the money." "I'm not spending my hard-earned cash on that video game." "You need to save some of that money you got for your birthday.") Your dialogue has to include clarification, explanation, and instruction. Remember, what you don't teach them at home they will learn somewhere else, and money is one of those intriguing topics that *will* grab their attention if they hear someone else talking about it. So, if you don't want Little Mary whose mommy and daddy teach her that it's okay to buy whatever you want on a little rectangular plastic card teaching your little one the same idea, be proactive! Talk to your children and live responsibly in front of them. They are watching you.

And speaking of that little plastic card, as early as three years old, children begin to notice that every time they want something you go into your wallet and pull one out. As a consequence, they begin to associate their wants with your debit or credit card. They don't understand that your card has a limit. They believe, like all children until they're taught differently, that money flows endlessly based on what you want to buy.

You might even hear Junior say, "Just use your card," or "You always have money." That's what my kids always tell me. And when I tell them money is low I may as well be speaking in tongues. The day your kids tell you to "just use your card," it's time to start the financial education process. Year four or five is the ideal age to begin teaching them; that is, school age. Have conversations about how money is earned and how to value it as soon as they have some conception about what it is.

Start by teaching them responsibility. Give them chores and let them earn an allowance. Assigning chores shows the child that you have to work to earn money, that nothing is just given. This will also help them to understand that their parents work to earn the money they use to pay bills, buy food, clothing, and the other things they need.

When you determine what the chores are, create a chart and place it on the refrigerator, or in some other highly visible area. Check off chores as they are completed, which will help hold them accountable. I recommend letting the allowance amount be based on their age. For example, if they're five, they get $5 based on the parents' pay period (weekly, bi-weekly, monthly). When you start giving an allowance, make it a big deal and be consistent. After all, how would you feel if you went to work for two weeks and didn't get paid? Or, your pay was short? Teach them consistency and reliability by demonstrating it.

Next, open up a student account (with you as the main account holder of course), at your neighborhood bank or credit union. At most financial institutions, you have to deposit ten to twenty-five dollars to open up a student account. While you're there, introduce them to the bank manager to begin teaching them about building relationships. I have been banking at the same bank since I was thirteen years old.

When they get their first allowance, teach them to incorporate the same method you are using at a much higher level mentioned in chapter one. They should allot 10 percent for their tithes, 10 percent should be deposited into a savings account, and the other 80 percent they can spend on items they choose. Weeks they have no items they want to purchase, have them put a higher amount in their savings account.

John D. Rockefeller created the three jars approach: save, spend, and share. Of course you don't have to use jars; you may prefer to use three shoe boxes, or three plastic containers. Whatever you decide is best, just label each one. I recommend you do the same for yourself but with one for your tithe, one for your savings, and one for your spending.

You'll also want to teach your kids the difference between needs and wants. Permit them to buy what they want as long as they allocate their resources to the two necessary jars first: their tithes and their savings. In times when there is nothing they want or need, encourage them to add more to their savings. Sometimes they will want something that they don't have enough money for. This is your opportunity to teach them about borrowing money and how to pay it back in a timely fashion.

Purchase them a wallet so they have a safe place to hold their cash. When you go shopping with them, allow them to pay at the register, so they get comfortable with handling money. Have the cashier count the dollars or change out, and make sure you tell your kids the importance of verifying the amount of money they receive back after they buy an item. (This will also sharpen their math and on-the-spot calculation skills).

When they're approaching their sixteenth birthday, begin teaching them the importance of credit. Tell them how essential it is that they guard their name, character, and reputation, in every area, but for the purposes of this lesson, specifically money. How many of you would agree that if you would have learned some of these tips at an earlier age you would have made a few different choices? How many credit card offers would you have passed up if you'd known the trap that was being set for you? Or, if you did get the credit card, how much less would you have charged? You would've probably only purchased the items you needed, and of course, you would've paid your bill on time every month. Make sure they understand that credit is not free cash; it is simply the ability to purchase something and delay paying for it till later.

If we don't teach our kids the ins and outs of credit, know that by the time they get to college, the credit card companies will be waiting for them. Since 2010, when the Credit Card Accountability,

Responsibility, and Disclosure Act (CARD Act) went into effect, it created some protective measures for college students, such as disallowing freebies like gift cards and t-shirts to be given away as a way of enticing students to sign up. Since then, the number of students getting credit cards is declining but it's still in the millions, which is still far too high when you consider that a large percentage of that number are uneducated about how to wisely use credit.

There are certain questions that you can teach your kids to ask (and questions you should also ask when you're considering applying for credit) and what answers they should look for concerning credit cards.

- What is the annual percentage rate (APR)?

- If there is a promotional interest rate for the first few months, what will it increase to once the introductory period is over?

- What is the credit limit?

- Is there an annual fee?

- Is there identity theft protection?

Credit card companies can be slick too, and because most freshmen (and alumni) lack knowledge about the credit card industry, they don't read the fine print and disclosures attached to all offers. (Note: Always read the fine print and disclosures!) When you don't, on average you will pay in the 15-27 percent range in interest rates, in addition to a high annual fee.

Help your child avoid destroying their credit and their name by teaching them the gospel of responsibility. In college, only one credit card is necessary. With it, they can establish credit at a young age, which is a good thing. Remember, the length of your credit history is a considerable fraction of your credit score pie.

Here's a little cheat sheet of finance topics you should teach your kids about:

- Understanding Money and Its Value

- Paying Tithes

- Saving: Creating Great Habits

- What It Takes To Earn Money: Hard Work & Responsibility

- How to Make a Purchase/What Things Cost

- Setting Financial Goals and Budgeting

- Paying Bills and Borrowing

- Understanding a Credit Report And How To Establish, Build, and Maintain Credit

- Prioritizing Financially: Needs vs. Wants

AFTERWORD

I spent my entire adult life laboring in a nationally recognized community development financial institution. Now retired, I find it ironic that I would be penning the same message I used to proclaim some sixty years later—a message that totally agrees with the author —that a man bound by debt is shackled to a life of fear and bondage. Whereas, a man who uses his money wisely, no matter how little or much he makes, looks to the future with expectancy and optimism, unfettered by money issues. He is not only an asset to his family, but an owner and a builder of his community. He is respected by all those he comes in contact with and leaves a legacy behind for others to appreciate and follow.

Obtaining financial freedom doesn't require lots of money, nor an MBA. It simply requires making wise decisions, educating oneself on the sensible use of credit, spending less than you earn, putting God's portion first, and saving for a rainy day.

Some years after joining "THE WORD" Church in Cleveland, Ohio, I was pleased to meet and work with a God-fearing young man who held the position of CFO. He was assisting the senior pastor, Dr. R. A. Vernon, in doing some amazing things in the community. I quickly recruited him to share his expertise with Faith Community United Credit Union, the inner city financial institution I was in charge of at the time. That young man was LaRese Purnell.

After only a few short interactions, I came to realize that LaRese has a heart for people. I witnessed him serve tirelessly in ministry, freely using both his education and experience to share with others what they needed to do to be better financial stewards.

That information is now in your hands, literally. With his advice, in time, you too can and will be financially free.

While sitting in a Birmingham jail, Dr. Martin Luther King Jr. wrote:

"We are caught in an inescapable network of mutuality, tied in a single garment of destiny. Whatever affects one directly affects all indirectly."

Your decisions today will affect your posterity tomorrow. It's important that we learn how to make wise financial choices early, correct mistakes and erroneous thinking as soon as we know better, and share what we learn with those whom we love to prevent them from making costly mistakes as well.

To that end, *Financial Foundations* is an invaluable resource. It is a toolkit of timely, relevant, and useful material, providing the information you need to make sensible financial decisions.

I urge you to immediately put into action what you've learned, one tool at a time. It may well change your life and the lives of those around you for generations to come.

Rita L. Haynes, CEO Emeritus
Faith Community United Credit Union
Cleveland, Ohio

APPENDIX A

———

The list below states what documents you need to have on hand. I recommend you purchase a small fireproof safe to store these documents. It would be costly and time consuming if you had to replace them.

Document Storage
Short Term Emergency Documents
Birth/death certificates
Social Security cards
Passports
Emergency contact information (insurance agents, doctors, family)
Marriage certificates/divorce decrees
Wills and/or Power of Attorney
Copies of your driver's license, green card, and other identification cards
List of bank account and credit card account numbers
Long-term Documents
Tax returns

Credit card statements

Medical records

Retirement savings statements

Investment records

Bank Statements

Pay stubs

Legal documents

Bills

Warranty/rebate documentation

APPENDIX B

As items expire based on the retention schedule make sure you shred to avoid identity theft.

Document Retention Schedule	
Documents	**Length of Time**
Tax documents	Keep tax returns, as well as supporting documents like W-2 forms, receipts, and real estate closing statements for seven years. The IRS may audit you within three years if it suspects good-faith errors; six years if it believes you underreported your income by at least 25 percent; and unlimited time if you did not file a return or filed a fraudulent one.
Investment records	As long as you own, plus another seven years. Need them to prove capital gains and losses.
Bank statements	One month. Due to them being available online for up to six months to a year.
Retirement plan statements	Most, one year, for tax purposes. Keep Roth IRA statements until you retire, to prove you already paid tax on your contributions. Based on institution you can review quarterly statements online.

Credit card statements	Review for fraudulent transactions then shred and retrieve quarterly statements from online as needed.
Paychecks	One year, until you receive your W-2. To verify last stub with W-2.
Bills	One year, for deductions on taxes.
W-2 forms	Until you start drawing social security for verification of eligible income.

40 MUST KNOW
FINANCIAL BUZZ
WORDS

---

1. **401k Plan** – A qualified retirement plan through an employer to which eligible employees can make salary deferral (salary reduction) contributions on a post-tax and/or pretax basis.

2. **403(b) Tax Sheltered Annuities** – A qualified retirement plan for eligible employees of public schools, tax-exempt organizations and eligible ministers; Similar to a 401k plan but mainly for non-profit organizations.

3. **Amortization** – The paying off of debt in regular payments over a period of time.

4. **Annuity** – A financial product designed to grow an individual's funds and then upon annuitization, pay a fixed payment for the designated number of periods. Annuities are used primarily as a way to secure cash flow during retirement years.

5. **APR** (Annual Percentage Rate) - The annual cost of a loan including all fees and interest, expressed as a percentage.

6. **APY** – Annual Percent Yield- The annual return of an investment for a one-year period. This rate includes compounding, which

makes it greater than the periodic interest rate multiplied by the number of periods.

7. **Asset** – Any resource that has economic value that an individual or corporation owns. Assets are generally viewed as resources that produce cash flow or bring added benefit to the individual or company.

8. **Bankruptcy** – A legal proceeding in which a debtor's assets are liquidated and the debtor is released from further liability.

9. **Bond** – A debt instrument used by corporations, governments (including Federal, State and City) and many other institutions that are used to generate capital. The investor does not become part owner like a shareholder, but does have a greater claim on the issuer's income than a shareholder.

10. **Capital Gain** – A capital gain is realized when an investment's selling price exceeds its purchase price.

11. **Cash Flow** – One of the main indications of a company's overall financial health; calculated by subtracting cash payments from cash receipts over a period of time (month, quarter, and year).

12. **CD** – Certificate of Deposit – Interest bearing note offered by banks, savings and loans, and credit unions. CDs are FDIC insured and provide interest on the investor's money that is locked in for a certain term (usually three months to six years).

13. **Compound Interest** – Interest that is calculated not just on the initial principal but also on the accumulated interest from previous periods. As interest is added back to the principal, the rate of return applies to the entire balance, making the balance grow even faster than simple interest (simple interest is when

the interest is applied only the initial principal, not the accumulated interest as well).

14. **Coverdell Educational Savings Account** – A replacement to the Educational IRA, the Coverdell ESA is a savings vehicle for parents to use for their child's education. Though contributions to the account are taxed, earnings used for educational expenses are not. The funds within the account must be used for qualified educational expenses before the beneficiary's thirtieth birthday. Taxes and penalties may apply if distributions are not taken properly.

15. **Credit Report** - A summary of a person's credit history, showing historical information such as bankruptcies, loans, late payments, and recent inquiries. Individuals can obtain one free credit report from each of the three credit bureaus each year.

16. **Credit Score** – A measure of credit risk that is based on activities such as credit use and late payments. Credit scores can be obtained for a fee from one of the three credit bureaus. One of the most common credit scores in the U.S. is the FICO score.

17. **Debt** – An amount owed to a person or corporation for funds borrowed.

18. **Delinquency** – When a borrower fails to repay a debt obligation by the agreed term.

19. **Diversification** – Spreading risk by investing in a range of investment tools such as securities, commodities, real estate, CDs, etc.

20. **Garnishment** – A legal process whereby a debtor's personal property is seized in order to satisfy a debt or court award.

21. **Inflation** – The gradual increase or rise in the price of goods of a period of time.

22. **Interest** – The fee paid for using other people's money. For the borrower, it is the cost of using other people's money. For the lender, it is the income from renting the good (the money).

23. **Keogh Plan** – A pension plan for self-employed individuals or employees of unincorporated businesses. It is also known as self-employed pension.

24. **Liability** – An obligation to repay debt.

25. **Liquidity** – The ability of an asset to be converted to cash quickly without sacrificing value or giving a discount on the price.

26. **Loan-to-value** – The ratio of the fair market value of the asset to the value of the loan used to purchase the asset. This shows the lender that potential losses may be recouped by selling the asset.

27. **Mutual fund** – An investment that is made up of a pool of funds from multiple investors who want to invest in securities like stocks, bonds, money market accounts, and other assets. Mutual funds are operated by money managers who invest capital and try to create gains for the investors.

28. **Net worth** – Basic calculation of assets minus liabilities. Used both for corporations and individuals to measure financial health.

29. **Prime Rate** – Determined by the federal funds rate (the overnight rate at which banks lend to one another) the prime

rate is the best rate available to a bank's most credit-worthy customer.

30. **Principal** – The original investment on which interest is generally paid.

31. **Risk Averse** – An investors desire to avoid risk; a more conservative approach to investing is generally upheld by risk averse investors.

32. **RMD** – Required Minimum Distribution – The minimum annual amount required for retirement account holders to withdraw, starting at age 70 ½. This amount is calculated based on the account value on December 31st of the prior year divided by the factor on the IRS RMD table. (RMD does not apply for Roth IRAs.)

33. **Roth IRA** – Retirement vehicles that allow certain individuals who meet income restrictions to contribute funds that have already been taxed in order to save for retirement. The withdrawals from Roth IRAs will never be taxed (including interest – after five years of the initial investment).

34. **Share** – One unit of ownership in a corporation, security, or limited partnership.

35. **Stock** – A proportional share of ownership of a corporation. A company may offer one-hundred shares of stock and if you own ten, you have 10 percent ownership of the company.

36. **Tax-deferred** – Postponing taxes until a later date – common tax-deferred vehicles include IRAs, 401k, and Keogh Plans, 403(b), and pension plans.

37. **Traditional IRA** – A retirement vehicle that allows you to save pretax funds for retirement. These funds are taxed upon withdrawal and may be subject to penalty if withdrawn before age 59 ½.

38. **Yield** – The annual rate of return for an investment expressed as a percentage.